"In *Flashing Bugs,* walk in Kerr's shoes as a
parent of a child with a life threatening illness.
His moving, year-long narrative will wrench
the heart of every parent. In Kerr's recounting
of his daughter's illness, the steadfast strength
of family and friends brings welcomed warmth
and richness to the story. This book should be
read by all those who treasure families and appreciate the blessings of good health and great
doctors."

- Dolph C. Simons III, President -
Newspapers Division, The World Company

"Engaging, honest, and soulful, *Flashing Bugs*
is a riveting meditation on family life in a time
of crisis. Should be required reading for any
parent who's ever wondered how they're going
to make it through the next day, not to mention
the next year. I couldn't put it down."

- Whitney Terrell, author of
The King of Kings County

Flashing Bugs

By
Whitney E. Kerr Jr.

Edited by
Diane McLendon

Cover Design by
Zach Swanson

Cover Concept by
Whitney E. Kerr III

Book Design by
Tom Dolphens

Published by Rockhill Books,
an imprint of Kansas City Star Books
1729 Grand Blvd. Kansas City, Missouri 64108

First edition.
Softcover ISBN: 978-1-61169-056-9
E-Book ISBN: 978-1-61169-065-1
Printed by Create Space.

ROCKHILL
B O O K S

Flashing Bugs

By
Whitney E. Kerr Jr.

CONTENTS

Part one
A Rude Awakening
Early May, 1993

●

Part two
The Deluge of Treatment

CONTENTS

•

Part three
Survival and Recovery

•

Epilogue   163
October 25, 2010

Foreword

What's it like to have a child with a life-threatening illness? Most of us have no idea until it hits us. My wish is that this story might in some way give comfort to those in crisis. Maybe it will prepare them for what's to come. Maybe it will help them realize that others before them have run the same gauntlet. And maybe it will give them hope.

Like most amateur projects, this would not have come together without the assistance of many fine people. Barbara Bartocci helped me early on with editing. Payson Lowell offered me some good advice on publishing. Laura Dail, literary agent in New York, also gave me some advice on structure and format. Drs. Craig Satterlee and Kathleen Neville supplied me with medical terminology. Debbie, my wife, and our children frequently helped me overcome my clumsiness on the computer. My assistant, Carolyn Kulash, was always available to handle details in the home stretch. Finally, Doug Weaver and my editor, Diane McLendon with Kansas City Star Books, provided guidance and helped get it into its final form. Cheers to you all!

FLASHING BUGS

To Mika, Jimmy, Jamelle, and all the
others ...

FLASHING BUGS

Part one:
A Rude Awakening
Early May, 1993
Chapter 1: Ill Wind a Blowin'

"Girls, be careful here. You fall in, you gonna' get all wet and dirty."

The quiet stream meandered its way through the woods. On rainy days past, it had violently slashed its way through the soft soil like a jagged knife. But right then it wasn't deep or dangerous, just tempting to little people. Charlotte and Mariella, at four-and-a-half and almost three years old, acknowledged my warning with giggles.

Life had crept back to the gently rolling countryside of Arrow Rock, Missouri. Though spring usually arrived in early April, the bright green foliage still looked new after a harsh winter that finally said farewell just weeks ago. Living in the Midwest, we tried to convince ourselves how fortunate we were to have the change of seasons, but we still cursed our luck at the extremes. Spring and fall were glorious but too short. Winter and summer punished us. Those who could afford it went north to Lake Michigan in the summer and to Florida for the winter. We who stayed got through it because we knew it would change. With that change we found relief and validation.

"Shall we, Professor?" I asked.

"Let's do it, Professor," answered Rick, as we stepped into the timber.

One form of relief from winter's cruelty was the springtime ritual of morel mushroom hunting. Our morel search called for a five gallon bucket, a long stick to poke through the May apples, and some "Deep Woods Off" to repel the ticks. It always took a few minutes for my eyes to adjust. The mushrooms' spongy texture and earthy color made for great camouflage. One minute I could stare right at a cluster and not see them. A moment later they stood out like thistles in wheat. During their brief season they would change from smallish and gray in early April to large and camel colored in early May. The old-timers said that the best time to hunt was near the full moon when the evening temperature stayed above 60 degrees. The weather needed to be moist and humid; the heavier the better. Finding them was the challenge. Some people favored apple orchards while others preferred river bank sycamore trees. Others swore that a dying elm held the most promise because the golden age of morel hunting occurred at the height of the Dutch elm disease in the mid '60s and early '70s.

Morels were one of the few good things to come from that plague. It decimated the elm trees which arched over the streets of old Kansas City like giant cathedrals. Block after block after block. I remember as a little boy living on Huntington just west of Wornall Road. A river of black beetles assaulted the giant elm in our front yard. Thousands of them poured out of a hole in the trunk. We children tried spraying them with a hose, but it was to no avail. The tree died.

As we searched through the forest, we gradually separated – Rick ventured off by himself while Charlotte and Mariella clung to me like cockleburs. The woods could intimidate little children. The combination of thick brush, bedtime stories like Hansel and Gretel, and strange sounds gave this spot an eerie feeling.

"Any luck, Professor?" I called.

"Not yet, Professor," answered Rick.

Rick saved the "Professor" designation for his favorite people. If he addressed you that way, it meant you were a good guy and he liked you. He would then go on to explain that "Professor" was a name usually reserved for the piano player at a house of ill repute. At this point he would break up with laughter. The idea of calling such a musician "Professor" always struck him as very amusing. As his son-in-law, I now returned the favor.

In 30 minutes, we'd almost walked in a circle when we reached a clearing near the creek. Charlotte and I were still engrossed in the hunt but Mariella was getting bored. The sudden "kerplop" of a frog diving into the water got her attention. Fascinated with every kind of insect and animal, this little girl was determined to get acquainted with that frog.

"Daddy, Daddy, I found one!" squealed Charlotte.

"Let me see, sweetie. Where is it?"

"Right here. See?" She pointed to it. Yes indeed! It was a magnificent morel, a sturdy six inches tall.

"Way to go, Charlotte," I complimented. "Professor, your granddaughter found one first. Look at this thing. It's enormous!"

Rick ambled over with a big smile across his face.

"Let's see it, Professor." His expression changed to amazement at the sight. "Oh my goodness, Charlotte. You found this on your own? What a great hunter you are!"

Charlotte smiled and laughed.

"I found the first one, Daddy."

"You sure did, big girl," I responded. "Now remember, when you find one, there should be several more nearby."

Searching the ground as I spoke, I spotted another and then:

"Here's one!" crowed Rick.

As he picked it, he was careful to leave the base of the stem in the soil. Removing the entire mushroom supposedly prevented the remaining spore from growing back. Besides, the stems were no good for eating. Like they did sometimes, the morels now came into view all around us. This was the moment of the hunt for which morellers dream – when mushrooms seemed to appear everywhere and all at once.

We were picking handfuls when we heard it. It was the

sound of a large splash in the creek – the kind of sound that could only be made by a three-year-old like Mariella who'd lost her balance and fallen into the muddy water. Rick and I looked at each other.

"Uh oh, Professor. I think we have a problem."

"Indeed, it seems our little friend has taken the plunge, Professor," Rick replied.

Mariella's cry confirmed it. She was standing waist deep in water, streaked with mud and soaking wet.

"I fell in, Daddy," she blubbered between sobs.

"You sure did," I agreed. "How'd that happen?"

"I wanted to play with the froggy."

The frog had escaped Mariella. Somewhere deep within the psyche of that little three-year-old girl was disappointment not only with falling into the creek but also from rejection by a frog that didn't care to make her acquaintance.

"I want to go home! Please, Daddy. I wanna go home!"

We took Mariella up the road to the Townsend house where my mother, Day Kerr, helped me clean her up and get some lunch. I dumped the morels out of the bucket into the sink where I rinsed them off with water. Though I didn't know it then, our morel hunt would be our last truly carefree excursion for the rest of 1993.

Our family felt fortunate to have a place in the country near Arrow Rock. My parents first began to acquire the farm in 1980. Three miles west of the little town and an hour and a half from Kansas City, it now included three dwellings – the Greek Revival "Prairie Park" which dated back to 1844 and neared the completion of a major restoration, an adjacent guest cottage, converted from what had once been slave quarters, and the antebellum Townsend house which was where my brood liked to stay.

The village of Arrow Rock was once a bustling river town and political center with a population of more than 1,000. In 1860 more than 70 riverboats stopped there each week. All that changed a few years later when the Missouri River channel shifted course. The town was suddenly two miles from the waterway and no longer a functional port. But in time this "Williamsburg of the West" overcame the river's betrayal and reinvented itself as a tourist destination and an important link to the past. The entire township was designated as a National Historic Landmark with restaurants, antique shops, bed and breakfasts, and the Lyceum, one of only three repertory theaters in the state.

The Missouri River is mercurial. She gives and she takes away. From St. Louis to Omaha there are more than 400 known riverboat wrecks. And now – almost 150 years later, nothing has changed. In spite of the efforts of the Army Corps of Engineers to dredge the river and build massive levees, she still gets out of control and goes on a rampage. The ancients would describe her as a temperamental goddess committed to punishing us from time to time for our disrespectful encroachments across her sacred river valley. Soon she would administer her next round of punishment.

It all began later that night. After returning from Arrow Rock to Kansas City, Charlotte became ill, vomiting several times. The sickness continued with fever through Sunday. My wife, Debbie, and I took her to the emergency room and returned home with a diagnosis of the flu. The flu in May? The same symptoms persisted into Monday when our pediatrician, Dr. Nirmal Mitra, decided to check Charlotte into St. Joseph Hospital in South Kansas City. Just four months earlier I had rushed Debbie to the same St. Joseph Hospital where she gave birth to our twin boys, Whitney and Carter. But in January, we had known what to expect at the hospital. Now we had no idea.

Our lives, up to now, had moved along smoothly. By 1993 Debbie and I had been married six years. Both of us had grown up in Kansas City, gone away to college, and returned home. We loved it here. My family, the Kerr's, went back seven generations.

Like my father, for whom I was named, my career was in commercial real estate and I depended on commissions for my family's livelihood. I couldn't afford to neglect my clients, even with a sick child. So while they ran more medical tests, I drove to Riverside, Missouri, to inspect the new warehouse space I'd leased for the O'Rourke brothers.

When the phone in my car rang, I answered distractedly, preoccupied with work. As soon as I heard Debbie's voice, I knew something was wrong.

"The doctors think her appendix has ruptured," she answered. "How soon can you get here?"

Suddenly, I felt the burn of prickly heat. Real estate no longer mattered. I could only think of Charlotte, suffering in the hospital. A ruptured appendix could mean death. Nothing was more important than getting to the hospital right away. I squashed the accelerator of my Oldsmobile Ninety Eight as I raced away from downtown on Southwest Trafficway.

"I'm on the way right now."

"Be careful, honey." Debbie warned.

Out of nowhere I abruptly thought of my late grandfather, Everett Gibson. He was killed in a car wreck in the 1930s while rushing to see his mother. Somebody had told him she was dying and to get there quickly. A tire blew and he never made it. In a cruel case of irony, his mother survived. He left my grandmother with two children and one on the way. At the time, my mother was only two years old. So I was careful, but still, I made the 30 minute drive in less than 20 minutes.

Debbie and Mitra were waiting with Charlotte for Dr. Ron Sharp. Mitra felt it was important that we have Sharp involved because he was the top pediatric surgeon in town. We grew impatient as we waited – wondering why he would leave us in limbo while Charlotte's condition grew worse. Mitra had to leave. I'd always thought that a ruptured appendix was a serious emergency, where every second was critical. Didn't

Sharp realize that she could be dying? Minutes passed. Followed by an hour.

"What's taking this guy so long?" I griped, pacing back and forth across the room.

"I know, Babe, but Mitra said he's the best. He'll be here. Let's just try to relax. Dad's planning to stop by later this afternoon."

"These damn doctors are all the same. It's like nobody outside their profession has anything to do but wait around all day."

I realized I'd better be careful. Debbie didn't like criticism of doctors. Her father, Rick, was a cardiovascular thoracic surgeon. One of the things I loved about Debbie was her intense loyalty to family and friends. She was quick to the defense when someone close came under attack.

"Knock it off, Kerrdog. He's busy. If he's as good as Mitra says, it's worth it. Don't you want the best for Charlotte?"

"Kerrdog" was a nickname I picked up in college and had not been able to shake. The word "cur" is defined as a mangy mutt. Hence, Kerrdog.

"Deb, I get it. Okay? But how good is it for her to just sit here? She needs attention now. A ruptured appendix is serious."

"Why don't you go get a magazine at the gift shop?"

"Yes, dear."

Two of the most frequent and painful words a married man must utter, but I was getting nowhere with the complaining and she was right. So I left to follow the advice of my wife, a doctor's daughter.

But when he finally showed up late that afternoon, even Debbie had grown impatient. We were irritated and skeptical. Kind of like when you're at a restaurant and hungry, you've waited a long time, and when the food finally arrives, you wonder if it will be worth the wait. With his tweed jacket and bushy mustache, Sharp looked more like an ivy league professor than a hotshot surgeon. Based on first impressions, the plate was large but the serving was small. After we made our introductions, he got right to the point. He could sense our anxiety.

"This isn't an appendicitis attack," he said. "You don't need to worry about that. Charlotte's symptoms don't support it. We'll run some more tests and figure it out. Relax." He smiled as he said it, looking back and forth at us and Charlotte as he gently stroked her head. "We will take good care of our little girl here."

It was nice that he had finally made an appearance but we were still in the dark. If I had been thinking more clearly I would have pressed him. After waiting all afternoon, we wanted answers.

He left us and we felt some relief but if the problem wasn't her appendix, what was it and when would we find out? An ultrasound test later that day revealed what looked like a pocket of gas in her abdominal area. The technicians had a difficult time reading the screen.

A CT scan the next morning confirmed the presence of a "mass" near Charlotte's stomach. This would generally mean a cyst or a tumor of some kind. At this point we had reached the limits of care St. Joe Hospital could deliver. The St. Joe staff and Sharp told us that we needed to transfer Charlotte to Children's Mercy Hospital for further examination. Children's Mercy specialized in pediatric care, especially the difficult cases regular hospitals couldn't handle.

It was all tumbling along so quickly. Neither Debbie nor I clearly understood what was happening. But we sensed something sinister was at work. As we left the hospital and drove downtown toward Mercy, I noticed ugly dark clouds forming to the southwest. That's where our weather always came from. It was still tornado season. I wondered if the weather was an omen.

Chapter 2: Shock of Ages

At Mercy we were introduced to Dr. Arnold Freeman, a pediatric oncologist. At the time, I didn't realize that oncologists dealt with cancer. Freeman was accompanied by Cathy Burks, the senior nurse specialist in the oncology department. Freeman was 60-ish with spectacles and thinning black hair. He spoke in a brisk, businesslike manner, an abrupt departure from the laid back style of Sharp. I felt uncomfortable with him right away. I could sense that Debbie wasn't too thrilled either. We were seated in a cramped and stuffy examination room. They had already run several tests on Charlotte. Freeman made no time for small talk.

"Based on the test results, I believe that your daughter has a tumor, and I think it's malignant."

Bam! It felt like the time I got smacked over the head with a beer bottle after work at Louie's Bar and Grill as a summer construction worker during college. But this news about Charlotte was a different kind of jolt. It wouldn't wear off in a few hours. My head spun. In the space of only a few days, Charlotte had traveled all the way from an upset stomach to a deadly disease, from the peace and tranquility of Arrow Rock to the cold reality of cancer.

Freeman continued, "In my opinion, this tumor is what we call a neuroblastoma, an aggressive and fast growing type of cancer. We need to take action right away."

Debbie and I felt numb. Cancer was something that attacked adults – not four-year-old girls. Charlotte was too young. How was this possible?

"Well, um … uh … Dr. Freeman, w-what exactly do you mean by action?" I stumbled.

"We'll need to remove the tumor surgically and follow that with intensive chemotherapy and radiation."

This was one of those moments that left most people speechless. And we were. Hit by so much so quickly, we had to learn more about cancer before we could come up with questions or comments. It all needed to sink in. How could he know so much at this point? We'd only just arrived that day. I felt dizzy, like the passenger in a fighter jet screaming along at Mach Two. The world was flying by and I was powerless to do anything.

Burks looked at us with sympathy. I sensed that cancer upset her. This was the part of her job that never got easier – delivering bad news to young families and turning their world upside down. Kind of like the detective who has to knock on somebody's door and tell them that their loved one has been murdered. What a horrible job – the messenger of bad news. I reasoned that she was there to support us and perhaps to counterbalance the blunt, cold-fish approach of Freeman – no easy task as far as Debbie and I were concerned. I didn't pick up any empathy from him. It seemed as if, in his mind, Charlotte wasn't a child. She was a case, just another project to keep him busy. To him, taking care of her was no different than solving a complicated equation. How were we going to deal with this guy? It seemed like he had no heart.

"We need to take you for a tour of Four North," Burks interrupted. "That's our oncology ward. It's where you and Charlotte will stay while she undergoes treatment."

"How long will her treatment last?" I asked.

"It could take a year or more," answered Freeman, "We really can't say at this time."

We left Charlotte back in the room with one of the nurses. She was resting and comfortable.

Patients at Mercy came from throughout the Midwest and from all walks of life, from the inner city to rural countryside to affluent suburbs. Yet everybody was on an equal footing. Treatment was the same, regardless of one's ability to pay.

When we stepped onto Four North that first time, we entered a world that was strange and frightening. The place was full of children with many different forms of cancer. How could there be so many sick children? Where have we been all these years so unaware? And this was just the cancer ward.

It was bustling and noisy. There was the beeping of monitoring equipment, televisions playing cartoons, and intermittent crying. There were nurses, doctors, interns, and assorted staff members moving all at once in different directions with their shoes squeaking on the white linoleum floor. There were parents and volunteers who moved at a slightly slower pace. Most notable were the patients, bald headed children with pale skin. Some were in little red wagons propped up with pillows. Others moved about on their own. All were connected to IV trees on wheels.

There was no real privacy, I quickly learned, when our entourage marched unannounced into a corner room.

"Meet Jessica," declared Freeman, in his abrupt way. It was like he was showing us a lab specimen – not a living, breathing little girl. "Jessica, would you please show these people your Hickman."

It was more like a command than a request. Jessica was a cute little redhead about ten years old. Without hesitation she lifted her shirt to reveal a meshy garment strapped around her upper chest to hold her Hickman catheter in place. The Hickman catheter was surgically implanted into her chest; a tube inserted into the right atrium of her heart to deliver chemo drugs and intravenous fluids.

"Your daughter will have one of these when she gets out of surgery. We'll show you how to take care of it," instructed Freeman.

Jessica smiled at us as we filed out and then went back to reading her book. Apparently it was nothing unusual to have a group of strangers walk into her room. First, most rooms were double rooms – shared with other families. There were only a few private rooms for use by those patients with seriously weakened immune systems who needed isolation in order to avoid the deadly threat of infection. Second, since Mercy was a teaching hospital, there were constant groups of medical students who followed the doctors on their rounds. While the doctors conducted examinations of the patients, they also made comments, passed on pointers to their students, and answered questions.

After the tour of Four North, we were escorted to a regular room on the second floor of the hospital where Charlotte had already been checked in. This would be her room until results of her surgery officially confirmed that she had cancer.

"Or that she did not," I thought, clinging to hope.

Debbie and I sat in silence for a long time.

"Dr. Freeman seems to have it all figured out, doesn't he?" I finally asked.

Debbie didn't much care for people like Freeman who had such negative thoughts and opinions. She refused to see things pessimistically.

"I think he's gotten a little ahead of himself," said Deb. "How you feelin' sugar?" she asked Charlotte as she sat next to her on the bed, rubbing her back.

"I wanna go home," was Charlotte's answer.

So did I. There was nothing to prepare us for something like a child with cancer. Nothing like this had ever happened in either of our families when we were growing up in Kansas City. I didn't remember this with any children I knew in school. None of our friends had ever dealt with it. It was totally foreign – one of those awful things that you heard about with other people but was now happening to us. There was no instruction manual for dealing with it. We would have to navigate our own way through this medical maize.

Rick stopped by to visit. At a time like this, it really helped to have a cardiovascular surgeon as a father-in-law. After we relayed the conversation with Freeman, he was thoughtful.

"Nobody knows enough at this point to say for certain that it is cancer," he said. "We won't know until they examine tumor samples taken during her surgery." Rick's calm demeanor was reassuring but it meant that we were still in limbo until after her operation.

The uncertainty of not knowing made the waiting for answers much more difficult. And abruptly, the rush of the whirlwind practically stopped. Time barely crept along. Our lives were moving in slow motion. I felt boxed in and trapped. Almost paralyzed.

A little later, Sharp returned to check on Charlotte. This was the first time Rick had met Sharp. Their discussion was fascinating but somewhat incomprehensible – laced as it was with medical jargon. They both took an optimistic approach to the surgery which was scheduled in just two days from now, this coming Friday morning.

"My thinking is that this will more likely be a teratoma than a neuroblastoma. And teratoma are generally benign," ventured Sharp.

The description of a teratoma conjured up gruesome images. A teratoma could actually be a failed mutant twin.

"This thing could have been with Charlotte since she was in the womb. Sometimes they have tissue, bone, hair, and even teeth. But, as far as this Friday's surgery is concerned, I'll be in and out in no time," he said. "It'll be a chip shot."

And with that he smiled and departed.

Now there was nothing for us to do but wait until Friday. Charlotte had stabilized and wasn't in pain. The uncertainty gnawed at us through the next day. Although nobody really knew what the problem was, word had spread among friends and family. Everybody had been helpful around the house and with our other children, Mariella, Whitney and Carter. My mother and Debbie's mother, Sally Ramos, split time taking care of the children. Debbie had been with Charlotte nonstop. So, in two days we'd have a much better understanding of Charlotte's condition. The only catch was that Sharp had underestimated the difficulty that lay ahead with this simple, little chip shot.

Chapter 3: Chip Shot from Hell

On the morning of the surgery, I made it to Mercy by about 7:15 a.m. Debbie and Charlotte were up and cheerful. Charlotte was scheduled to go into surgery at 8:00. Earl Cavanaugh, the Dean of Grace and Holy Trinity Cathedral and our pastor, was with us as we left the room and headed to surgery. I had no idea at this point how tough and difficult a day this would be. Debbie and I both leaned over to give her a hug and a kiss.

Daily we said farewell to those we expected to see tomorrow. There weren't many times when we wondered if it was the last goodbye. It made me realize how much I took for granted those daily farewells. Nothing seemed certain anymore.

Charlotte cried and called out for us when she realized that they were taking her away. Watching my four-year-old daughter roll away to surgery was sickening. Was this the last time I'd see her alive? The surgical nurses, in their scrubs festooned with cartoon characters like Mickey Mouse and Donald Duck, guided Charlotte's gurney toward the ominous double doors that led to an operating room and the great unknown.

Cavanaugh was a bear of a man at six feet and six inches tall. He draped his massive arms around us and said a brief prayer for Charlotte. Debbie and I both took a deep breath, wiped around our eyes, and moved on to the waiting room where we found our entourage: Rick and Sally, my parents, Earl's wife Nancy, my sisters Mary and Bess, my aunt Mary, Debbie's sister Adrianne, and our close friends Mitch and Jennifer, Fritz and Rosie, and Ellen. During the day my brother-in-law, Joe, dropped in along with another pal, Willie.

The waiting room atmosphere started off fresh and cheerful with everybody optimistic for a quick and successful outcome.

As time passed the seats were less comfortable and tension built. Magazines and newspapers grew tiresome. We found ourselves going back and rereading them on the chance that we had missed something the first time through. Empty coffee cups and food wrappers piled up and became irritating. Our clothes which felt clean and fresh began to stick and sag. Gradually, we all felt the need to get up and move around but there was nowhere to go. Our collective supply of small talk had run dry. We were caged up and ready for the release of good news like the surgery was over and she was going to live. And still, the hands on the clock just crawled. How could time pass so slowly? It was like waiting for the bell to ring in grade school.

Later we learned that Sharp had no clue to the extent of the "chip shot" he had in store until little Charlotte was laid out on the operating table, relaxed and completely anesthetized. Amid the bright lights and beeping of monitors he carefully ran his hand across her abdomen. That was when he felt a massive lump around her belly button. It was much larger than the scans had indicated. This simple tumor resection had suddenly become much more complicated. The procedure took place as follows:

"Uh-oh," he thought to himself. He opened her up with an incision that stretched from her sternum to well down below her navel. He was assisted by a junior associate and Tom Holder, the senior member of Mercy's surgical staff.

Nobody spoke when they first gazed upon the softball-sized tumor before them. It had completely enveloped her pancreas and pushed her intestines aside. Sharp's mind raced as he plotted his course to remove this monstrosity and save the life of a four-year-old girl.

The tumor had not only invaded the pancreas but, based on his initial observations, it probably extended into the liver. To most surgeons it was a hopeless situation – inoperable. At this point, the associate, spoke up, "Ron, there's nothing we can do here. We're way too late. Let's zip it up."

"Not so fast, Igor. We can fix this. And we will." Sharp replied.

"Fix it? C'mon Ron, this is unresectable. Look at the relative mass. It's throughout the lower abdomen. We do this
we'll wreck her vitals. Send her back to oncology for pre-op
chemo. Let Freeman shrink it and we'll come back in a few
months when there's some elbow room. Besides, what about
the spillage?"

"We'll minimize spillage with an auto transplant. And by the
way, you talk about late? If we wait for chemo, she's dead."

"Tom, you're awful quiet. If you have any thoughts, let's
hear them."

"Ron, I learned a long time ago not to doubt you. But you're
talking about a very difficult retroperitoneal procedure. Getting every bit of the tumor is one thing. Losing her on the
table is another."

Retroperitoneal means going behind the peritoneum which
is the membrane that lines the abdominal cavity. It's much
more difficult to get to than the abdominal cavity itself.

"I understand. Thanks, Tom." He turned to the head surgical nurse, "We operate now and we're going off site. Set us up
for auto transplant, stat."

Then he looked at his associate and Holder.

"Thank you, gentlemen. Now let's get to work."

In this instance, the auto transplant technique involved removing the abdominal organs en block and setting them on
a separate operating table where the surgeons would dissect
the tumor away from the vitals and then reset the same organs
back into the abdominal cavity.

This was Charlotte's first bit of luck in the past week – getting
a surgeon skilled and gung-ho like Ron Sharp. There were
very few surgeons capable of doing what Sharp was about to
attempt. Sharp was a devout Mormon with five daughters and
one son. Maybe he looked down at Charlotte and saw one

of his own children on that table. Who knew all the thoughts that go through the mind of a pediatric surgeon? Apparently, he dealt with these impossible situations on a regular basis.

What is it that determines the difference between surrendering and fighting on?   Some people are wired to push themselves harder than everybody else. Later, we would realize that when Sharp took your case, you had a big advantage. We were lucky to find Sharp in the first place. It wouldn't have happened without Mitra. Maybe "inoperable" was a relative term. What really mattered was who wielded the scalpel.

Meanwhile, our group in the waiting area talked and read. We tried to stay upbeat but as the day wore on and more time passed, we felt more uneasy. This wasn't going as expected. The worst part of the day came when Dr. Tom Holder, Chief of Pediatric Surgery at Mercy and Sharp's partner, entered the waiting area at about 2:30 in the afternoon to give us an update. Charlotte had already been in the operating room for more than six hours.

Holder was an icon at Mercy and approaching the end of a very distinguished career. He was raised in Mississippi and carried himself like the southern gentleman he was. As we gathered around him in his green scrubs, I sensed from the look on his face that the situation was serious.

Looking at Debbie and me he said, "Your daughter is holding up very well. We've had to remove about 80 percent of her pancreas and," he paused slightly, "it appears that a portion of the tumor is malignant."

This was not what we had had hoped for. Dammit! Freeman was right. Now our Charlotte was in really big trouble.

He continued, "We also tested the lymph nodes and the portal vein. The portal vein is important because it leads into the liver. The lymph nodes were negative but it appears that the tumor has also invaded the portal vein. The toughest part of the surgery is over but it'll take us a while to put her back together. We'll be back to you before too long."

Our worst fears were now realized. The cancer nightmare had now begun. Sharp finally came out after finishing – about 7:00 p.m. He looked amazingly relaxed after what must have been a grueling day.

He held up his pinky finger and said, "Charlotte's pancreas was about this big before today. I had to remove most of it but I left the head. That should be enough for her to produce insulin on her own."

"Did you get the whole tumor?" I asked.

"Most of it. Even though it completely enveloped the pancreas, we got all of it there. But it also breached the portal vein."

He sat down and grabbed a piece of paper to sketch it out for us. In his drawing the cancer looked like a cluster of grapes.

He continued, "The tumor was wrapped around the portal vein and penetrated a very small section. I didn't think it was necessary to go all the way into the portal vein at this point. We did remove some of it. What she went through was traumatic enough. Besides, we can get the rest with chemotherapy."

"How's Charlotte?" Debbie asked.

"Well, she's had a rough day but she should be fine. All her vitals are stable. These little children are tougher than you'd think," he said with a smile. "We also put her Hickman in."

I guess   that was Sharp's way of saying that the surgery phase of this adventure was likely done but the chemotherapy, what we would come to realize as the protracted phase, was about to begin.

Debbie spoke up again, "So does Freeman take over from now on?"

"That's the way it works. He'll oversee things from here."

"We're not too sure about Freeman. He's so negative."

Sharp looked down at the floor for a moment with his hands clasped. Before he responded he cleared his throat.

"Debbie, I have six children that I love very much. If any one of them had cancer like Charlotte, I'd want Freeman handling it. He's the number one pediatric oncologist in the city and he's the best chance your daughter has at surviving this."

Sharp had made his point. Charlotte's survival was what really mattered. Personalities and such were irrelevant. The big question was whether or not we could keep the cancer from spreading into her liver. At this point we had to expect that microscopic amounts had already done so. Charlotte had indeed come through the surgery very well. Blood loss was not substantial. She received only one unit of blood during the twelve hour operation. The surgical nurse led us into recovery to see her, our little bundle of four-year-old wrapped up in bandages and hooked up to numerous tubes, sleeping comfortably. Debbie reached down to stroke her bangs. I stood behind Debbie with my arm on her shoulder. I wanted to hug Charlotte but I was almost afraid to in her condition. She seemed so fragile. She would spend that night in the intensive care unit and if her recovery continued as planned, she would move to Four North the following day.

Although we were tired and the cancer had been confirmed, we felt positive. We spent that night at Mercy. We squeezed into Charlotte's pre-op single bed since Charlotte was in the ICU. We fell asleep immediately. The next morning the ICU nurse reported how later that evening Charlotte had asked to watch cartoons. Then, at the end of the night, she asked the nurse to climb into bed and hold her. The nurse obliged. Mercy was a special place. The nurses treated the patients like their own children.

Chapter 4: The Limbo Walk

The day after the surgery, I went home to take care of household chores. Our home was in Brookside, a friendly urban neighborhood on the Missouri side of State Line Road. We did not have a big yard, but lawns of any size needed attention, so I planned on getting out the mower. But the lawn had already been cut by our next door neighbor. The next day, fifteen women were in our back yard, sweeping the patio, planting flowers, and making things look nice.

Babysitting and meals were taken care of into the next several weeks. One of the strengths of Kansas City was that we helped each other in times of need, even those we did not know. It was an important part of the Midwestern spirit which hearkened back to pioneer days when we circled the wagons in times of trouble.

As a commissioned salesman, I was used to taking care of myself. In business, I didn't expect people to do me any favors. But now that the word had gotten out about Charlotte, so many people – even some we didn't know well – reached out to us. The offers of help and kindness were overwhelming.

Likewise, Charlotte's hospital room was filled with balloons, pictures, and cards; a colorful poster from her pre-school; and books and presents from so many people. Parked at the door was one of the little red Radio Flyer wagons which the hospital provided so parents could pull their children around the halls and, when the weather was nice, go outside for a breath of fresh air. Everywhere we went, of course, we had to take her IV stand. It was like a cloak tree on wheels. The IV was sustaining Charlotte with nutrients while she was unable to eat solids.

Charlotte had recovered very well from the operation and didn't seem to have developed any serious complications. But we had not yet received any diagnosis on her specific type of cancer. This one was a mystery and that was one of the trying aspects of this ordeal – the uncertainty and the waiting that went along with it. When we sat at St. Joe Hospital waiting for Sharp or when we agonized through the lengthy surgery, it seemed like we spent so much of our time waiting and wondering. What was wrong with Charlotte? What was it called?

How long would it take to treat her? What were her chances of survival? How often did children get this form of cancer? The questions piled up but nobody had the answers and all we could do was keep waiting and hoping. So there we sat, stalled in a medical purgatory.

And, though her recovery had gone well, Charlotte hurt and asked us to hold her. It was tough to see her in so much pain, but at the same time, I was amazed to see her alive after what she endured. As a layman, it was mind boggling that there were those among us with the skill and emotional control to disassemble another human being and then put that person back together, especially when it was a little child. I could barely change the oil on my lawn mower.

Charlotte continued to improve but her spirits weren't as high as we would have hoped. Normally, she was so cheerful and bubbly. Now she was mad at what had happened to her. Her anger had boiled over into several outbursts which prompted us to schedule a meeting with one of Mercy's child psychologists. What could we do to improve her behavior? My sense was that she would get better once we brought her home. But Charlotte's amylase and lipase were elevated. This was related to inflammation around the pancreas from the surgery, which affected her insulin production. This meant she had to continue the IV for nourishment. No solid foods until the amylase and lipase dropped. And until she started eating solid foods, she couldn't leave the hospital.

Debbie soothed Charlotte and did what she could to help her cope.

"We'll go home soon, sugar. Just as soon as you can eat on your own. Hang in there, baby. Momma's here with you. I love you."

She was so good at giving comfort. I marveled at her endless supply of loving patience, not only with Charlotte but with all of our children – especially when they felt bad.

My mother had finally run out of gas taking care of Whitney and Carter, our three-month-old twins. So, it was my turn to take care of them. The boys and Mariella had been shuttled around hither and yon over the past week. They had stayed with my parents and also with Rick and Sally. It was best that they get back home to familiar surroundings and a regular routine. At least one would have thought so. But that night was a new low. Mariella and the boys fussed all night. They had all developed colds with bad coughs. I only logged a total of three hours sleep.

Another cloud on our personal horizon was the tug Debbie felt, pulled between wanting to be with Charlotte and not wanting to spend too much time away from Mariella, Whitney, and Carter. And Four North was not a restful place. Another patient and that child's family were sharing the room. Doctors and nurses walked in at all hours.

"Time for another stick," sighed Charlotte, as she grew more accustomed to the routine of patient life. This meant frequently having samples drawn, paying for answers in blood.

And there was no way to get more than one or two hours of uninterrupted sleep. The hospital provided recliner chairs with vinyl upholstery that folded out for sleeping, but they were very uncomfortable, like seats on an airplane. And like an airplane flight, Debbie was thrown together with strangers in cramped conditions hoping to arrive in good health, trusting the flight crew who in turn relied upon the air traffic controllers. As passengers stuck in a holding pattern, we felt lost in the clouds.

Chapter 5: A Diagnosis (At Last)

Children's Mercy had never seen a cancer like our daughter's. Charlotte had pancreatic adenocarcinoma or pancreatoblastoma. Pancreatoblastoma was extremely rare. There were only a handful of cases in the last 20 years – worldwide. What was difficult to diagnose would likely be difficult to treat.

There was no treatment protocol. We had very limited in-formation. At the other end of the spectrum, Charlotte had a form of cancer that only a handful of pediatric oncologists ever encountered during an entire career. To his credit, the pathologist at Mercy, Dr. Zwick, had never diagnosed it be-fore. He had to consult with his counterparts at Barnes Jewish Hospital in St. Louis. That's why it took so long for the official diagnosis. Once we knew the type of cancer, we needed to learn all we could about the best way to fight it.

Although the cancer cells had probably migrated into her liver in microscopic amounts, Sharp didn't want to operate again. Earlier he had indicated that he might need to take Charlotte back into surgery Friday or Monday to remove the cancerous portion of the portal vein. Subsequent tests of the portal vein tissue confirmed the malignancy. However, after further consideration, Sharp and Freeman agreed that it would not be necessary to go through the trauma of surgery in order to remove something which they could eradicate just as effec-tively with chemotherapy.

At the same time, our good friends, Michael and Joe Jack Merriman, introduced us to Dr. Art Elman of St. Luke's Hos-pital. Elman was a radiologist and had treated Joe Jack dur-ing his recent bout with stomach cancer. Since that time, the Merriman's had quietly given substantial sums to fund can-cer research around the country. Elman helped them identify worthy researchers, and as a result, Elman and the Merriman's had developed a strong relationship. Art volunteered to help arrange a second opinion with Boston Children's Hospital. Something this rare warranted special attention.

It was nothing against Mercy or Freeman. We wanted to make sure that we were getting our daughter the best treat-ment possible, and this was the first time either Freeman or Mercy had dealt with Charlotte's type of cancer. Besides, El-man already had a trip to Boston planned for other medical matters. I procured some of Charlotte's slides from Zwick and dropped them by Elman's house so that he could take them with him the next day. Elman was very sincere and took an interest in my family. He asked me about Debbie and our children. I also gave Elman a copy of Zwick's pathology report. He commented that Zwick had done a fine job.

The recovery continued. Charlotte couldn't eat but the IV kept her fed. She maintained her weight. In a strange way, we'd settled into the hospital life. I stopped by in the morning on my way to the office and again on my way home at the end of the day. Debbie had only been away from Charlotte and the hospital twice in all this time. It had already begun to wear on us and we had just started.

On May 21st, we assembled for the big briefing with Freeman about his proposed treatment. Freeman still didn't have much in the personality department. Debbie didn't like him because of his cold approach and the blunt way he addressed us at the first meeting when we toured Four North. Later he upset her even more when he confirmed that the tumor was malignant. She had nobody else with her at the time and they were out in a crowded hallway where everybody could hear the bad news. Debbie felt that he should have delivered the message to her in private.

After the episode in the hallway, it seemed – for just a moment – that he was trying to be friendlier. Maybe he sensed Deb's antipathy or perhaps Cathy Burks had whispered in his ear. Debbie had gotten acquainted with Cathy and liked her. My parents and several nurses were present as he began.

"Dr. Freeman, do you mind if I tape this meeting," I interrupted, "I'd like to share this with my father-in-law, Dr. Ramos."

"Oh no. Not at all," he replied. Freeman looked around the room and continued, "I would propose that we have an intensive eight month chemotherapy program with a second-look surgery at week ten. We will use a combination of seven different drugs including interferon. We will also administer the drugs intra-arterially. We need to be very aggressive with this. After the second surgery we should probably have radiation treatments over eight to 12 weeks. There is no protocol for this type of cancer. It's extraordinarily rare. We've never seen it before."

"What kind of side effects can we expect?" asked Deb.

"Her hair will fall out. The chemo will make her nauseous and give her fevers. She will get skin rashes and intestinal problems like diarrhea. The biggest challenge we'll face is that she will grow very weak from the chemotherapy. When that happens, her immune system cannot protect her from the flu or a cold. That's the time when she will be at the greatest risk and those of us caring for her have to be most vigilant. She'll have nothing left to fight an infection."

"Dr. Freeman," I interjected. "If Charlotte's cancer is so rare, how were you able to develop such a specific treatment program? What's your basis for it?"

"While we've never treated it here, we have been able to access a good amount of case history. There are about 20 known cases worldwide. We have actually gathered information on cases from as far away as France and Japan."

"I know it's a guess on your part, but Debbie and I need to understand what Charlotte's up against. What are her chances for survival?"

"From what we've learned and seen in those other cases, I think she has a 50 percent chance of survival."

"How can that be? I've heard that pancreatic cancer is basically a death sentence. Only one or two percent ever survive it."

"That's with adults. This is a children's version, which is incredibly rare and much different. It's not the same thing that attacks adults."

Later, after he had a chance to review the tape, Rick said he was impressed with Freeman's presentation. Now, we finally had a plan to counterattack this disease. For the first time in a long while it felt like we were making progress.

Chapter 6: Food for the Dog

On the real estate front, I had an encouraging new development with my entrepreneur friend, Richard Thompson. Richard founded the American Italian Pasta Company and now had a new business idea: Thompson's Pet Pasta Products. His big "aha" moment came when he watched his dogs gobble up bowls of pasta left over from a family dinner. He realized the dogs loved spaghetti as much as people did. This new pasta project was a sure winner.

I had shown him several manufacturing sites but nothing caught his eye until we crossed the Kaw River into a part of Kansas City, Kansas, known as "Armourdale." Suddenly Richard pointed.

"That's what I'm looking for!"

The building was a newer, precast concrete structure on a large tract of land. It was vacant. I thought he might like it.

"That's the Cedrite building. It's about 80,000 square feet on ten acres. Owner's a guy named Wilhite who owns buildings in this area. He built it for Cedrite. They went bankrupt. Now he's got the building back."

"What's he want for it?"

"Oh, I'd guess at least a couple million. But he's generally not a seller. He's probably got a good bit more than that in it, too."

I'd never met Wilhite. He had the reputation of a hardass. I tracked him down on my car phone and two minutes later a dark Cadillac sped across the gravel parking lot spewing dust into the hot humid air. Wilhite, along with his son, Billie Junior, led us through the big empty building. After the tour, Richard and I walked off by ourselves to discuss things.

"What do you think?" I asked.

"This would work - but not a penny over two million."

We walked back over to the Wilhites, who were waiting patiently. I addressed the elder Wilhite.

"Bill, it's gonna take a lot of money for Richard to make this thing work. This whole area was under water during the flood of '51. We've also got concerns about those railroad tracks causing access problems. So what's it gonna take to buy this jewel?"

It's always best to get the other party to set the price.

Wilhite stared at me with one of those "I hate brokers" looks.

"That flood was before you were born, young man. If you'd buy yourself a new pair of eyeglasses, you might notice there's a levee over there today. Like you, it wasn't here then either."

He was wound up tight. He did not like me.

"And we really don't want to sell. This is one of our nicest buildings."

"Well, you heard it, Richard. I guess we better go to the next building."

"Yeah, Whit, we'd best move on." We both turned and headed to the car.

"Whoa! Hold on a minute, fellas. We're just talkin'. What's the big rush?"

The sweat was pouring off his forehead. He tried to force a smile but gave up. It was just too hard for him. As he talked he looked at Richard – not me.

"My loan on this is $2,250,000. If you want to take care of your pal here, I'll need $2,400,000."

He looked at me when he said that.

"Yeah right, Bill," I thought to myself.

Ah yes. Listen to it. I could hear strains of violin music wafting across the catfish laden Kaw River from that spot where the stockyards once stood. Now it was just weeds sitting atop what some would say is at least 15 to 20 feet of compacted cattle manure. But that music … It was so sweet. Somebody get me a Kleenex. If he says the loan is $2,250,000, it's probably only $1,500,000.

Sometimes brokers banter about the price, but there are moments when it's time to make the deal. This was one of them.

"Richard wants to see a couple other buildings. But he could make this work. He will pay you two million tops, and that includes a four percent fee for yours truly. I'm cutting you some slack on the commission. I could have asked for six."

"Gotta take care of my agent, Whitney," interrupted Richard as he winked at the group. "I'm ready to do business but Whitney's right. We are looking at several other buildings."

Wilhite may have had a gut feeling that we didn't really have any better options but he wasn't willing to lose somebody like Richard. In this lousy market there was no telling how long it might be before the next good buyer showed up. I could tell he was angry. He was one of those guys accustomed to having his way, and he didn't like his negotiating position, especially when he had to pay a broker. Suddenly he reached over and grabbed his son, Billie, by the ear.

"Get over here, dumbass," he barked, pointing to some weeds in the parking lot. "Maybe if you paid more attention to the way things look, we could get people like Mr. Thompson to offer us more money, damn it! Well, c'mon now. Do you have anything to say? Look at this goddamn mess! How the hell am I supposed to count on you when this shit happens?!"

Billie just stood there, embarrassed, while his father glowered. The old man knew better than to rant at Richard and me so he unloaded on the kid. I interrupted his diatribe by looking at my watch.

"Bill, we're on a tight schedule. You wanna sleep on it or should I draw up a contract?"

He glared at me, looked over at the building, and then turned to Richard.

"Go ahead. But hurry it up before I change my mind. You

aren't the only game in town."

As we drove off I grinned at Richard, "Well, boss, welcome to Armourdale."

Chapter 7: The Hickman

On May 22nd, it was my turn to spend the night with Charlotte. At last, Deb could go home to be with Mariella, Whitney, and Carter. Charlotte and I both slept well. Sometimes, at the center of the crisis – here at the hospital – I could forget about everything else and just focus on Charlotte. It was like the calm in the eye of the hurricane. I would get to Mariella, Whitney, and Carter as soon as I could, but at the moment, I needed to take care of Charlotte.

"Good morning, Margie," I said.

"Good morning, Kerr's."

Margie, a vivacious redhead, was one of our favorite nurses on the staff. She carefully scanned the IV machine and checked Charlotte's vitals. This morning she was here for more than a routine check-in.

"Attention, Dad. We need to clean and flush Charlotte's Hickman. You need to watch this and learn because you and Debbie will have to do it when Charlotte's back home."

As a non-medical person, the Hickman catheter and the idea of caring for it were daunting. Essentially a shortcut to the heart, the Hickman could do many good things like deliver IV fluids, drugs, etc. But, mishandled, it could just as effectively transfuse lethal germs or disease.

I went around to the other side of the bed and stood next to Margie so I could watch the procedure up close. The point at which the catheter entered the center of the chest was always covered in order to protect against infection. Proper maintenance required changing the bandage and cleaning the site at least weekly.

"Everything you'll need is in this kit," she said. "You can do this with or without gloves but the key is to keep everything clean. Wash your hands really well."

The neatly packaged kit included an assortment of disinfec-
tant swabs, wipes, and clean dressings. She wiped the slid-
ing meal tray with an alcohol soaked paper towel. Then she
washed her hands. Next she set out the contents of the cleaning kit on the tray.

"First we get rid of the old bandage," she said.

She removed it carefully so as not to tug on the catheter. It
was now pretty well anchored into Charlotte's chest by subcu-
taneous cuffs which absorbed body fluids and expanded after
initial insertion in order to secure the catheter in place and
prevent any movement.

"Then you need to wash your hands a second time. Look it
over to make sure there's no infection or anything that looks
strange."

"What if I do see something?" I asked.

"If that happens, you'll need to bring her in. Any infection
with this could be trouble. But like I said, if you keep it clean
and follow the directions, there shouldn't be any problem." She
gave me a reassuring smile. "Then we take the alcohol swab
sticks and wipe around the area where the catheter meets the
skin. Start at the center. Wash your way out in circles. Don't
go over the same area twice. Toss the used swab and repeat
the same two more times with the alcohol swab."

Charlotte stared up at us paying careful attention and lying
perfectly still.

I winked at her and asked, "Are you remembering all this,
sweetie? I'll need you to help me when we're home."

Charlotte looked up at me, smiled, and nodded her head.

"Okay Dad, ready for the next step?" Margie interrupted.

"I think I'm getting it. Carry on."

"We do the exact same thing all over again using the iodine
swab sticks. We also need to clean the catheter which we
will rest against her skin underneath the new bandage. We're
almost done. Take the pieces of gauze and gently wrap them

around the base of the catheter. Then cover it with the bandage like this."

She peeled off the tape which covered the adhesive edges of the transparent Tegaderm bandage and skillfully placed it over the sterilized skin. Finally she coiled the catheter and secured it to Charlotte's chest next to the new bandage with a piece of white medical tape.

"Well, that's it," she said. "Any questions?"

"I don't think I'll ever do it that easily."

She grinned. "A little practice and you'll be fine, nurse Whitney."

"Yeah, right. What about the flushing part?" I asked.

"That's lesson number two. Ready to learn some more?"

"Might as well, I guess."

"We need to flush the Hickman to keep it clean and prevent blood clots," she continued. "This calls for another kit which I just so happen to have in my pocket."

The kit she displayed was not as extensive as the first.

"Same procedure as before. You gotta keep it clean," she said as she removed the tape around the injection cap and cleaned the cap with the iodine wipe. "You need to let it dry for a couple minutes."

Next, she removed the needle cover on the syringe and inserted the syringe into the center of the catheter injection cap.

"Next I release the clamp like this. Then we inject the heparin. As we inject the last few cc's, we slowly remove the needle from the cap. Get rid of the old syringe, retape the cap, and we're done."

She made it look so simple and effortless.

"Are you going to give Debbie the same lesson?" I asked. "I don't want to forget anything."

"Don't worry. We'll go over it again before you leave," she replied.

After Margie left, I sat back in the bulky lounge chair, sipped coffee out of a Styrofoam cup, and ruminated. The real estate business had been awful. Here and across the country, real estate markets have struggled to overcome a devastating combination of the 1986 tax law changes and the savings and loan debacle. It really flew out of control after a regulatory investigation into Lincoln Savings and Loan that implicated five U.S. Senators ("The Keating Five"). After Lincoln collapsed, nearly half of all S & L's followed suit. Lending institutions were collapsing almost daily. Foreclosures of commercial properties were happening nationwide. There was weak demand for businesses looking to buy or lease space. Financing was only available for those who didn't need it. Many of the transactions I'd worked on had fallen through. General business activity seemed dried up. Many of us worried that our economy was in a death spiral.

I had no salary. I was on straight commission. I was a modern day gunslinger low on ammo. How would I be able to take care of my family? On top of it all, we had the huge disruption of Charlotte's illness. On the bright side, we did have good health insurance. Thank goodness for Blue Cross and Blue Shield. There was no way we could have paid for this out-of-pocket. Before her treatments were finished the cost would run into several 100 thousand dollars.

"Daddy, my tummy hurts," whined Charlotte, interrupting my meditations.

"I'm sorry, baby. You want me to go get Margie?"

"No," she answered emphatically.

She must have been in pain because in the last few days she'd had temper tantrums. She was tired of being caged up in this place where they bothered her constantly. At times she'd been very uncooperative with the nurses. Debbie and I were scheduled to meet with the child psychologist, Dr. Ross. What could we do to help her with the discomfort? Could we do anything to improve her behavior? Our sense was that things would get better when we brought her home. We wanted to take another trip to Arrow Rock before she started chemotherapy, but Charlotte had vomited twice in the past 24 hours. Mercy wouldn't let us take her home until the nausea stopped. So there we were, trapped in the hospital, grateful for the care, but wanting to get out. How much longer before we could go home?

Chapter 8: Escape to the Country

We finally figured out what was making Charlotte so miserable. She had a fluid accumulation around the pancreas. It was not draining and caused her severe discomfort and a loss of appetite. Also, she'd been having gas pains. We were caught in a digestive catch-22. She didn't feel like eating anything but until she started eating, we couldn't go home. Once again, I was at home and Debbie was at the hospital. The phone rang. I got to it after the fourth ring. I was in the middle of changing Carter's diaper.

"Good morning, Whitney. It's Art Elman."

"Dr. Elman, it's good to hear from you. Debbie and I want you to know how grateful we are for your help with the second opinion. We really appreciate it. Have you learned anything yet?"

"Well, yes." A slight pause followed. "Whitney, we've learned quite a bit. I wanted to report to you on what they said at Boston Children's."

There was hesitation in his voice.

"What's the matter? Did you get some bad news?"

"No, not exactly. It's just the feedback I'm getting from BCH. They have some concerns about what's proposed by Dr. Freeman. We think his plan is ingenious and extensive but, in our collective experience, we don't see how all that he recommends will be effective and safe."

"Are you saying that there is no point in doing chemo?"

"No. She definitely needs chemo. But BCH has seen two patients with pancreatoblastoma. They have some ideas on a scaled down version as opposed to Freeman's approach which is to throw everything at it and hope that something sticks. I really think you should go see them. I'll arrange it for you."

At that point it really sank in. We could never live with ourselves if Charlotte died and we'd passed up a chance at a second opinion, especially with BCH, a hospital which has seen Charlotte's cancer.

"You're absolutely right, Doctor. We've got to do it." I paused a moment and took a deep breath. "I really appreciate your taking the time to do all this."

I felt a lump growing in my throat. Why would a busy and successful doctor bother himself with our situation?

"No need to mention it, Whitney. I'm glad to help you and your family."

He was genuine. Elman's assistance was a reminder that the appearance of wealth often obscures the fact that most doctors truly care about people. I pictured his massive home on 56th Street just west of Ward Parkway. It was featured in a National Geographic article about Kansas City which appeared in the 1970s. But it really wasn't that complicated. Big house or not, people like Art Elman simply wanted to help. After all, he was in the business of making people get better.

We finally brought Charlotte home from the hospital that day. We planned to spend Memorial Day at Arrow Rock. The girls and I would go fishing and our reunited family could enjoy a long weekend together before the treatment began – in whatever form it took.

Before Charlotte's release, Freeman stopped by to check on her. Debbie and I needed to tell him about our decision to seek a second opinion and this seemed as good a time as any. I looked over at Debbie before I began and thought to myself, when we first met Freeman he was rather blunt and to the point. Turnabout was fair play, right?

"Dr. Freeman, we hope you won't take this the wrong way

but we've decided to get a second opinion. We're taking Charlotte up to Boston Children's Hospital. We understand they've actually seen a few of these cases."

I paused to gauge his reaction. Debbie and I had never been in this position before. We were appreciative of what he had done thus far, but based on his lack of experience with this type of cancer, we had no choice.

For a brief moment I detected a bit of surprise and maybe a trace of disappointment, but it quickly passed. He was composed and thoughtful.

He looked at us and said, "These little cancer cells are very clever in the way they hide and avoid the treatments we prescribe. They're diabolical – like the Viet Cong. We need to hit them as hard as we can the first time."

"Dr. Freeman," Debbie offered, "We just want to do what's best for Charlotte. Maybe we'll learn something useful in Boston."

"We couldn't live with ourselves if we didn't do this, Dr. Freeman," I jumped in. "They've actually treated this cancer before. Put yourself in our position."

"Please. Let me be clear. I have no objection to your seeking a second opinion. I completely understand. We all want what's best for Charlotte. It's just that there are lifetime doses of chemotherapy. Her body can only take so much of these drugs. If we don't get the maximum effect the first time around and the cancer returns, there may not be any way of stopping it the second time."

He'd made his point. But we were still going to Boston.

Before Boston, however, we had our weekend at Arrow Rock. It was such a relief to have Charlotte out of the hospital as we drove out of town. In college, I'd read Vergil's Georgics, which contrasted the serenity of country living with the harshness of ancient Rome and its multifaceted corruption. Though short lived, a weekend in Arrow Rock brought respite from the stress of urban life. Each year, I drew encouragement from the dependable way the country revealed its dark richness of freshly tilled soil, the latest generation of calves, and the hopes and potential of another year.

Our trips to Arrow Rock usually included fishing at several of the ponds scattered about the property. Saturday morning, Charlotte and I decided to drive over to the little ramshackle bait shop outside of Blackwater that sold nightcrawlers. The weather was balmy as we drove south on the gravel road with the windows of the Buick station wagon rolled down. Although she was no longer required to, Charlotte sat up high next to me in the child seat. She was smiling and happier than she'd been in weeks. She had on a cute little pair of pink sunglasses and her blond bangs danced in the breeze. She was so excited to be freed from Four North. As we drove we saw birds, rabbits, and deer. Observant as she was, she provided me with a running commentary on all the wildlife which appeared along the way.

I found myself glancing over at her several times. I ached for her to get well. Looking at her I was amazed at how alive she seemed after such a major surgery. I consciously locked away in my memory these images of her. However things turned out, this was one of those moments that would help me remember Charlotte as a happy four year old. I realized that up until then, my memories of her sort of ran together and were not as clear or precise as this one of her sitting next to me while we drove along a country road.

Later, on our way back with several containers of wriggling bait, we picked up two box turtles by the side of the road as a surprise for Mariella, Whitney, and Carter. Charlotte thought it was grand.

My brother, Gib, joined my parents and our brood later that day. We fished at the little pond by the abandoned one-room schoolhouse without much luck until heavy rains forced us to seek shelter. This was disappointing because that pond normally offered good action for bass and bluegill – especially right before a storm.

Sunday greeted us with steamy weather. We made an unproductive excursion to the big pond west of Prairie Park. We took Charlotte and Mariella but they didn't like it much. The grass around the pond was very soggy. It was like walking on a wet sponge.

Prone as she was to mishap, Mariella fell into a puddle and got mud all over her moccasins. For some reason, Charlotte was in a grumpy mood so I took them both back to Debbie and the boys at the house.

Deb and I both worried about Mariella because we didn't think she'd been getting her fair share of attention. The experts on parenting talked about how critical the early years are in a child's development. Since Charlotte fell ill, Mariella has been more rebellious. We thought a large part of this was due to Charlotte's illness, but we also thought it was her nature to be a little feisty. Meanwhile, Whitney and Carter were doing fine. All they did was eat, sleep, cry, kick, laugh a little, dirty their diapers, and eat. And they had each other.

Memorial Day brought another memorable moment with Charlotte. Overnight the temperature had dropped into the 50's. While it was cool and breezy, the clouds thinned out and made for a very pleasant day. Fortified with windbreakers, Charlotte and I went out to test the recently-repaired swing that hangs from the venerable pecan tree next to the circle driveway of the Townsend house.

My father was the one who fixed the swing. He and my mother spent almost every weekend in Arrow Rock. They loved the farm and the rich history of the area. My father kept himself occupied with numerous projects ranging from clearing brush to repairing old hardware and restoring antique furniture. He was an uncompromising perfectionist and stayed busy all the time. He often said that these projects gave him an immediate sense of accomplishment – a rarity in the real estate business where day to day progress was difficult to measure. It usually took months, even years, to close transactions.

My mother liked to relax a little more than Dad but there was also plenty for her to do around the houses and the garden. Actually, the farm had three houses – Prairie Park, the adjacent slave quarters which have been converted into a guest cottage, and the Townsend house just down the road about a third of a mile to the west.

As expected, the swing worked perfectly. After Charlotte had enjoyed enough of the back and forth, I suggested we try our luck on the big north pond. Gib claimed to have landed two nice channel cats there yesterday. So that she wouldn't tire out, I carried her down to the pond on my shoulders. When the first cast resulted in a thrashing two pound catfish, Charlotte's interest in fishing perked up. We then worked as a team. She would carefully reach into the Styrofoam container and hand me a worm. I would bait the hook and cast. We had instant bites. We caught lots of fish with the trusty old night-crawlers – bluegills, bass, and catfish – but the best thing was to see that spunky look of determination as Charlotte reeled in a healthy bull bluegill, laughing triumphantly. That fish was a fighter but he didn't stand a chance against Charlotte. I didn't want to be any place else other than fishing with her. Her illness was forgotten. Charlotte and I were together catching lots of fish and nothing else mattered.

Later, when we returned to the house, I took the catfish to a spot by the back fence where we cleaned our fish. It was downwind and far enough from the back porch that we wouldn't smell the guts and fish heads which we tossed into the pasture. There was also a faucet and hose for washing up. Our water came from a well deep in the ground. Cleaning catfish has never been my favorite pastime, but I wanted the children to understand the connection between the fishing rod and the dinner table. From the shed I grabbed a five foot long two-by-six board, a hammer, and a 16-penny nail. I placed the fish belly down on the board, careful to avoid the barbs on the side of the head which would give the careless a nasty jolt. Once I had it positioned, I drove a nail through the back of its head securing it to the board. Next, with a sharp knife, I made an incision all the way around the head from front to back. Using a pair of needle nose pliers, I peeled the skin down from the base of the head to the tail. The trick was to try and pull it off in one piece, but it didn't usually work that way as the skin tore and I ended up with several pieces before finishing. After yanking the skin away, I cut off the head. Next, I grasped the fish in my palm, stomach side up. I slid the knife into the vent and sliced open the gut all the way up to where the head had been. Then I removed the entrails and rinsed the cavity with water. It was ready for the skillet. Charlotte and Mariella watched the whole procedure. Mariella was fascinated but Charlotte was mostly disgusted.

On the drive back to Kansas City, before we hit the interstate, I spotted a deer running full speed through a pasture on an angle to collide with us. I had to hit the brakes as she sailed over a fence, landed in the middle of the road, stumbled, and ran on past us. Debbie and the girls were amazed at her athleticism. It was June, which meant the does were moving out of the timber and into the open pastures to give birth. The combination of labor pains and the instinctive urge to accelerate delivery made the does recklessly active.

Most people thought of November as the risky time on the road because of the bucks chasing after the does. But June was nearly as bad when it came to vehicles hitting deer. We counted six doe carcasses on the side of I-70. They had just recently collided with vehicles. Each was stretched out with her pregnant white belly exposed. The legs were bent and twisted unnaturally but pointed upwards, beseechingly, as if to ask, "Why must we die?"

I thought how sad it was to see innocent lives cut short. It reminded me of our own situation with Charlotte. I pushed the thought away and focused on the trip home.

That night, Rick and Sally came over for dinner. Rick would accompany us later this week when we went to Boston for the second opinion. Debbie and I felt very fortunate to have him along. He'd already been a great help to us through the early stages of treating Charlotte. At the end of the evening, I sent him and Sally home with two freshly dressed catfish.

Chapter 9: Wrecks in the City

It was 8:00 in the evening when I gazed out the Kerr & Company offices on the eleventh floor of the Brookfield Building – located at the southwest corner of Eleventh and Baltimore. It was growing dark outside. The wind wailed through the deserted streets like ghosts from the 1930s. Back then, Kansas City was considered the "Pearl of the Plains" and one of the most important cities in the United States. It was on full blast 24 hours a day, teeming with basement gambling parlors, or places like the Chesterfield Club where foxy waitresses wore nothing but high heels, and the throbbing Eastside juke joints powered by Charlie Parker, Duke Ellington, and all the other jazz greats. Not anymore.

During 1993, downtown Kansas City was a melancholy place. At the curb, newspapers swirled aimlessly. An occasional car or an empty bus interrupted the silence. Everybody else was now ensconced in the suburbs except for the after work boozers hiding out at taverns like "The Quaff" or those lonely souls who inhabited the grim brick apartments tucked away here and there.

I went inside them years ago, before developers revitalized parts of the area in an attempt to bring residential back to the urban core. As part of a community service project, I delivered meals to retirees who lived in cockroach infested flophouses, lit by the proverbial bare light bulb suspended from lath exposed ceilings. We had to be careful at the first of the month when they received their social security checks. Fueled by cheap booze like Thunderbird, they were all drunk, ghoulishly screaming at each other, fighting, or passed out. It was like a geriatric frat house except these poor souls had no future. That was 16 years ago.

Then from the street below came an eerie howl of despair. It was a derelict pushing a grocery cart full of empty aluminum cans. His cry had a piercing quality. I couldn't understand what he meant, but I felt the anguish and thought of the classic line of Henry David Thoreau: "The mass of men lead lives of quiet desperation, and go to the grave with the song still in them." He had long since given up hope that anyone would listen to him. He was screaming to himself.

For just a moment, I thought, there really wasn't much difference between that poor soul down there and me up here. I just happened to adhere a little better to the norms of society. But the precariousness of our existence ate at me. I saw how quickly the things I valued could disappear. Charlotte could die. The real estate business might get so bad that I could no longer support my family. Caught in a landslide of economic collapse, I could lose everything and end up like that desperate soul below.

The next day we would leave for Boston. What would Boston Children's Hospital have to offer us? Would we learn about the proper treatment? Did Charlotte really have a 50-50 chance of survival? When would we get a break from this oppressive uncertainty? I heard a distant siren. Time to go home. I slid some files into my briefcase and flipped the light switch as I walked out.

Chapter 10: A Difference of Opinion

On the day we left for Boston, Charlotte looked adorable in her blue and white-striped dress with a bow and a flower. She was wearing her black patent leather shoes with white socks. Debbie and I were so proud of her. Everybody at the airport noticed her and smiled. I think Charlotte picked up on it. She knew that in some way her princess-like appearance made those around her brighten up. The airplane ride was a big adventure.

Charlotte handled herself really well the entire day. It was not easy being stuck with grownups for such a long time. But something was bothering her.

As we neared the end of dinner and evening approached, Charlotte grew concerned and asked, "Daddy, can we please go see the ocean before it closes?"

We all chuckled but Charlotte didn't get the humor.

Debbie answered and hugged her, "Honey, the ocean never closes. It stays open all the time. I promise you will see plenty of it before we go back home."

The next morning we awoke to a beautiful, clear blue day. We were upbeat in hopes of finally learning how to deal with Charlotte's illness. We met the oncologist, Dr. Kupfer and the radiologist, Dr. Tarbell. Tarbell was Elman's connection at BCH. Apparently they went through medical school together and have since stayed in touch. Tarbell had helped to coordinate the second opinion in Boston.

The Dana Farber Cancer Institute at Boston Children's Hospital was a very busy place. People came here from all over the world. It was located in what could be described as not only the hospital district of Boston but also the medical Mecca of the United States – maybe even the planet. Right here were Boston Children's Hospital, Beth Israel Hospital, The Eye Infirmary, Massachusetts General, New England Deaconess, Boston City Hospital, Brigham & Women's, The Leahy Clinic, and so on. Also, there were three medical schools – Harvard Med, Tufts, and Boston College – not to mention Massachusetts Institute of Technology (MIT). The environment was extremely competitive and the best doctors in Boston were more than likely the best anywhere. It was the medical version of "Top Gun."

We met with the doctors separately as opposed to having them all convene as a group. We first met with Tarbell and then with the chief surgeon, Dr. Shamberger. Coincidentally, Shamberger grew up in Columbia, Missouri. How ironic it was that we came from the Midwest to get the very best advice only to find that a key member of the medical team was one of our own.

The BCH team recommended that we drop three of the seven drugs Freeman wanted and eliminate the intra-arterial administration of chemotherapy. Also, they didn't like the idea of a second-look surgery. They felt that CT scans would work better than exploratory surgery and be less damaging. Abdominal surgery leads to many complications such as intestinal lesions and excessive scar tissue.

Later, Rick told me how impressive Shamberger was, how good he had to be, and how hard he had to work in order to occupy his position as chief of surgery at BCH. We wondered how he managed to have any sort of a personal life away from the hospital. But most impressive were his comments on the work of Sharp. He couldn't have been more complimentary of Sharp's work during Charlotte's lengthy operation. Rick described it as "big time" in the minds of the Boston team. Although there were some differences of opinion as to what would be the best course of action, it was reassuring to have these experts speak so highly of Sharp and the outstanding work he did.

At this point our general feeling was that the program put forward by BCH would be more compassionate, less experimental, and just as effective. Their approach was to spare Charlotte from unnecessary pain and discomfort. In contrast, Freeman's regimen seemed harsher. The BCH program was based on the two cases they handled and the 20 similar cases known from around the world. They reiterated that this cancer was extremely rare. They proposed to use only those methods which had proven success. After lengthy discussion,

Rick, Debbie, and I felt very comfortable with the BCH recommendations but at the same time we didn't see it as a complete repudiation of what Freeman wanted us to do. We saw it as more of a fine tuning of what was put in motion back in Kansas City. Would Freeman see it that way?

Our next day in Boston started nicely, but ended on a very different note. In the morning, we took Charlotte to the Children's Museum and then we moved on to the New England Aquarium. The Aquarium was truly spectacular with its multiple exhibits and small aquaria on the perimeter of the main structure, which was built around an enormous cylindrical aquarium that extends upward almost three stories. The variety of marine life was mind boggling. Charlotte was filled with wonder. Somehow I couldn't help but feel a little sad that Mariella wasn't there. As much as she loved nature, she would have loved this place.

Then things changed for the worse. During the afternoon, when we checked in with BCH, we learned that their recommendations as relayed by Tarbell over the telephone were not well received by Freeman. According to Tarbell, Freeman had dug in his heels and would not agree to any of their proposed changes to the treatment regime.

The disagreement between BCH and Mercy was very troubling to Debbie and me. What should we do? Should we drop Freeman and engage somebody else? Should we switch to KU Medical Center or St. Luke's or perhaps even someplace in St. Louis? We liked the environment of Children's Mercy. How could we convince Freeman to adopt the BCH recommendations?

Rick suggested we take it one step at a time and postpone the debate on certain issues until they came up later in the treatment program. The second look surgery wasn't to take place for at least ten weeks, and the intra-arterial chemotherapy delivery wouldn't come into play for six to eight weeks.

The immediate question was the three drugs which BCH believed were unnecessary. Essentially, there were four drugs and radiotherapy which had proven effective.

The treatment would be debilitating enough with just the four drugs. And she would need all her strength to get through the reduced amount proposed by BCH. Why weaken her more with uncertain drugs? We've been told that the treatment itself actually killed many cancer patients. We should take the proven methods and hope that God would do the rest. If this didn't work, then we could take desperate measures. At that point there would be nothing to lose.

Debbie, Rick, and I carried on these discussions in front of Charlotte. Bless her little soul. She appeared oblivious to it – or so we thought.

Having concluded our consult with BCH, we decided to have a little vacation. Later that afternoon we drove north to Rockport and checked into a charming little bed and breakfast called the Seaward Inn. For dinner we rode over to Gloucester to a harbor side restaurant, Captain's Courageous, where we enjoyed a fabulous lobster dinner. From our booth, we overlooked the picturesque harbor and all the fishing boats.

"Mommy, what happens to us when we die," Charlotte suddenly asked.

There was a pause as Deb, Rick, and I looked at each other and then back at Charlotte.

"We go to heaven, sugar. It's a wonderful, happy place," answered Deb. "When we get there, we'll be with God and Jesus forever."

"Don't be too worried about that, Charlotte," I chimed in. "You won't be going to heaven for a long time from now."

"Right you are about that, Professor," echoed Rick. "You are very young, my dear. You have a big, long life ahead of you."

I didn't think she was asking the death question about herself but Rick and Debbie did. It was so difficult to gauge

the mind of a four year old – especially one as percipient as
Charlotte. The experts said that Charlotte and her peers were just
like little sponges soaking up everything they heard and expe-
rienced. But when it came to the really important questions
about our existence, how much really registered inside their
young minds? Mercifully, not a whole lot, I thought to myself
as I gazed at her. With her life in the balance and too young to
really comprehend or fear death, she smiled at me and sipped
away at her Shirley Temple.

"Charlotte, it's getting a little dark out. What time does the
ocean close tonight?" teased Rick.

"Popo, the ocean has no doors," she answered emphatically.

Later, after Debbie and Charlotte went to bed, Rick and I
watched the Chicago Bulls eliminate the Knicks on the road
to a third-straight NBA championship. This was now the "off
season" and we had the whole place to ourselves. I really enjoyed the company of my father-in-law. We smoked, sipped
scotch, and talked long into the night. It was now almost 2:00
a.m. Tomorrow we would go hunting for seashells with Charlotte on the rocky beach. It's something she's really wanted
us to do with her.

We savored a relaxing, carefree kind of day. Without a press-
ing schedule, we sampled the beaches and filled a couple
buckets full of seashells. Charlotte really enjoyed herself and
was especially fascinated with a tiny starfish we found in the
surf.

Charlotte seemed so happy and vibrant. I found myself
looking at her little smiling face, her bright brown eyes, and I
wondered, "Will she still be here two years from now?"

Such a morbid thought – the death of your own child   I
couldn't seem to shake it. It kept coming back to me – over
and over like the waves on the beach.

Debbie bought Charlotte two colorful hats with the idea that
Charlotte should get used to them because once the chemo

starts, she would lose her hair. Charlotte seemed to like a flowery, floppy one. She even put it on and wore it – on her own.

The trip to Boston was helpful in several ways. We established some common ground between the two approaches to Charlotte's treatment. We had peace of mind from knowing we sought out the best advice available. The journey also gave us a nice break from the grinding hospitalization of the past month and showed Charlotte a world bigger than Kansas City. And she learned the ocean never closes. That was the day that our "little escape" came to an end.

It had become unseasonably cold and rainy. From our big picture window, the waves smashed against the rocks as we packed to leave. Just as the weather had grown somber, we now faced the serious business of starting Charlotte's treatment when we returned to Kansas City.

Whitney and Carter.

Mariella and Charlotte with a catfish.

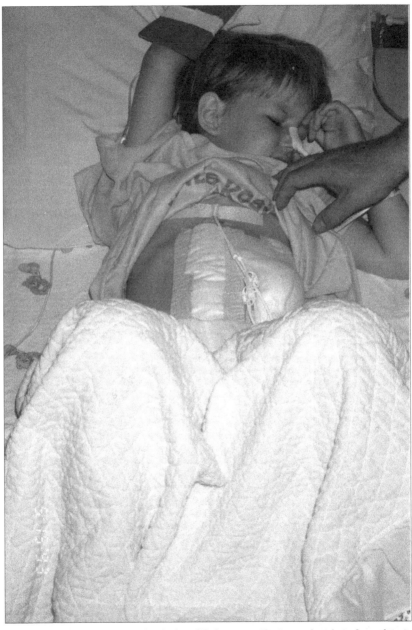

Charlotte after surgery - that's her Hickman catheter going into her chest.

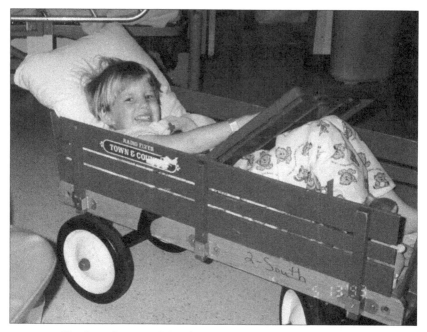

Charlotte in one of the Children's Mercy's Red Wagons.

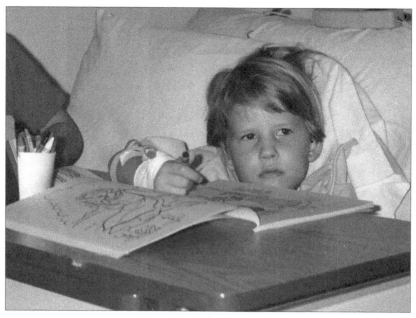

Charlotte in the hospital.

6-9-93
Charlotte in the hospital
bed

Mariella feeding the cows.

Rick, Charlotte, and me outside of Boston getting a second opinion.

Part two:
The Deluge of Treatment
Chapter 11: Round One — Greetings From Chemo Land

Freeman surprised us.

Debbie and I had prepared for a confrontation on the merits of his approach versus the Boston strategy. Perhaps it was divine intervention, but for whatever reason, Freeman acquiesced and agreed to incorporate the BCH treatment revisions. I'm not sure what it was that made him change his mind from when he and Tarbell had sparred over the phone. Maybe she had irritated him and he realized upon further reflection that he disliked the messenger more than the message. She did have a strong personality. From a professional standpoint, I knew he wanted the case. Debbie and I felt so relieved. At that point it really didn't matter what it was that had changed his mind. We believed that we had done the best we could for our daughter. As for the changes, there would be some fine tuning on the chemotherapy drugs. We would eliminate three of them. We would not utilize the intra-arterial delivery technique. And, we would take a "wait and see" approach to the second look surgery.

The first chemotherapy treatment began on June 7th. It was back to Four North for Charlotte and Debbie. They would remain there for the next four to five days as Freeman administered the first cycle of chemotherapy. Meanwhile, I would attend to things at home in Brookside on 65th Terrace, doing my best as a temporary single parent for Mariella, Whitney, and Carter.

That evening I called Debbie at the hospital to get an update.

"How's our patient?"

"She's doing fine so far. How's everything on your end?"

"I've got the children in bed. It's finally quiet. What else is new?"

"I had a nice visit with Freeman this afternoon."

"With Freeman? You're kidding, aren't you? I didn't think he was capable of that."

"He was great. There's a side to him you haven't seen. He dropped in and talked with me for more than a half an hour. We talked about his family. He has four children like we do. His are all grown up now."

"That's good. With all we've got ahead of us, we might as well have some detente. It's funny, isn't it?"

"What do you mean?"

"Growing up, I didn't like some kids until after we'd fought with each other. After trading a few punches, we realized it was much easier to be friends."

"Well, Babe, I don't know a whole lot about fistfights but I feel a lot better about Freeman."

His philosophy was to hit the cancer hard – not the patient. He was thinking about the future and he wanted a quality life for Charlotte five, ten, and 15 years down the road. We only had one really good chance to do this. As he had stated previously, there were lifetime doses of chemo drugs that a person could tolerate. If we didn't come in hard enough the first time and the cancer returned, survival was unlikely.

It was a big relief for both Debbie and me that were finally warming up to our oncologist. However, Charlotte didn't much appreciate him or Mercy. As far as she was concerned, she would rather be anyplace else. She was upset and disappointed about returning to the hospital for her first treatment, especially after the freedom and adventure of traveling to Boston. It was such a difficult thing for a little girl to understand – one day she was fine and the next day she was throwing up and had become very sick.

So far, Charlotte had received interferon, vincristine, and cisplatin. As I understood it, interferon reinforced the immune system. Vincristine came from the periwinkle plant and has been used for years in folk medicine. It's also what caused hair loss. Cisplatin was the nasty one of the bunch. It caused vomiting, possible hearing disturbance, kidney damage, and loss of appetite. We hoped it would equally wreak havoc on the cancer cells.

The distinctive Kansas City brand of humidity had settled in, making things hazy and uncomfortable. But it went even further. It sapped energy and dulled the mind. It made us lethargic and lazy. As in every preceding summer, it took us prisoner. Heavy air and oppressive heat wore us out like a ball and chain. The only difference was that this year it rained almost every day.

Late one evening, I was at home. The children were sleeping even though the weather was stormy. Late evening had become the time when I could relax. It was also when Debbie and I could catch up and compare notes. The phone rang. It was Debbie. She was crying.

"Deb? What's the matter? Is everything okay?"

"Charlotte asked Margie if she was going to die. She wanted to know if they would bury her in the ground."

She quietly wept. There was a long silence. With my other hand I scratched the hair above my forehead hoping it would magically release words of wisdom. I tried my best to comfort her, but nothing had prepared us to deal with a child who thought she was dying.

"Honey, it's gonna be alright. She's an intelligent, curious child. She asks questions about a lot of things." I went out on an advisory limb. "Try not to let it get you so upset, especially when you're around her."

"Duh … Don't be a dope, Kerrdog. I know that. I'm not with her right now. I'm down the hall in the parents' lounge." She continued, "It tears me up that our daughter has to think about death at her age. It bothers her a lot. I can tell it scares her."

"Honey, there's not much to say except that we're sorry she has to be there. The doctors and nurses are working hard to help her get better and we'll be with her all the way. Look, I know it's awful for you but we've got to get past this, okay?"

"I wish you were here with me."

"I wish so too."

"How are Mariella and the boys?"

"They're all sleeping, even with the thunderstorm. They must be getting used to thunder. Can you believe all this rain?"

"No. It's bizarre. At least the hospital stays aren't such a bummer when the weather's always crummy."

We continued with some talk for a few minutes and then said goodnight.

Chapter 12: Nightmare on 22nd Street

The chemo drugs began to take effect, and Charlotte started vomiting. She needed oral care four times a day in order to prevent mouth sores, which could lead to dangerous infections. It was hard to see our little girl decline so rapidly and uncontrollably.

As I looked at my sleeping daughter, I felt drained but somehow determined at the same time. The combination of caring for little children, trying to earn a living, and bouncing back and forth from home, hospital, and office had forced me to adopt a new attitude focused squarely on the survival of my family. I realized that caring for my family was the most important thing. Everything else seemed silly.

"I can't wait to get her home" seemed to be the mantra we used to get through the hospital stays. And home now meant so much more than a just a spot to plop down after a hard day at the office. Home was health and family togetherness. Home was where the world made sense and everything seemed to fit in place. Home was relief and refuge from all the awfulness out there.

Bringing Charlotte home from the hospital was supposed

to boost our spirits after the five days at Mercy getting chemo treatments. But Charlotte slept a lot, her voice croaked, she vomited repeatedly, and she had no appetite. We weren't used to seeing her so weak and lethargic. Mariella, especially, didn't understand. Why wouldn't her big sister play with her? The reality of what we would experience for the next year began to sink in. It was discouraging.

With the requirements of the portable IV and medicine dispenser, the anti-nausea condensation pump, and the Hickman catheter, Charlotte's care regimen required constant attention. Add to that the oral hygiene, side effects of the chemo, and other minor details like the love and care for three other deserving little children – the whole scenario bordered on the overwhelming.

Debbie and I argued more. Mariella, Whitney, and Carter were all in diapers. It seemed as if one or all of them cried constantly. If a recording of our children fell into the wrong hands, it could become a deadly new torture technique, I thought. And though I tried to shrug it off, our daily routine was punishing. When would we get a break? When would something good happen? I was beginning to think that our definition of "good" was when something worse hadn't happened. Cynically, I felt that happiness was just a temporary state of distraction.

Then I caught myself. In the strange nightmare on Four North there was ten-year-old Julie whose parents were helplessly waiting for her to die. Her head was horribly misshapen from incurable brain cancer. There was little three-year-old Dustin who had a neuroblastoma throughout his chest and abdominal areas. It was inoperable – even Sharp couldn't operate on it – but they hoped to shrink it with chemo. Then there was the 11-year-old from Joplin, Missouri. His name was Jimmy. He was mentally retarded. As if that wasn't bad enough, he also had cancer and had been undergoing chemo for several months. Each of these children was much worse off than Charlotte. Yet in spite of their overwhelming problems, they always managed to smile and even play. They ran up and down the halls like healthy, normal children. Somehow they had adapted.

When I found myself discouraged, I looked to Debbie. She had an unsinkable spirit. I believed that no matter how tough the circumstances, her ability to stay positive and care for Charlotte and the rest of our family would not change. Deb monitored Charlotte's blood count, tracking data on white count, platelets, and red cells in a daily notebook she shared with the staff. She took the lead in cleaning the Hickman and making sure that Charlotte was as well cared for as possible.

Parents needed to involve themselves in the day-to-day care of a seriously sick child. Mercy expected this. It was good policy. It made parents feel that they were doing something productive as opposed to standing by passively. By actively helping to care for our child we were, in a way, caring for ourselves. The busier we were, the less time we had to worry or get depressed.

We had to put Charlotte back in diapers because she refused to get up and go to the toilet. I fancied this was Charlotte's version of a "potty strike" in protest of childhood cancer. Maybe it signaled that she was getting better.

After two days, she abandoned her protest and asked us to help her into the bathroom. She had now officially renounced the diaper and the self pity which led her to it. Her natural feistiness had won out. This was a turning point. Here was the gutsy little girl we'd been missing. This was what had to happen. On her own, she needed to get mad and fight back. In a span of twenty minutes, she had us take her to the toilet three times.

But the next day Charlotte's white count dropped to 600. She had severe diarrhea and ketosis, a condition where the body wastes protein. Cathy Burks predicted that Charlotte would run a fever by the weekend. Then we would have to readmit her. Soon she would also need transfusions. We had in-home nurses slated to arrive tomorrow. Deb needed the help. Taking care of Charlotte in her weakened condition along with Mariella, Whitney, and Carter was more than she could handle. At least Charlotte could stay home for the next couple of days.

Chapter 13: Goodbye, Hair

Sure enough, Charlotte's temperature spiked to 101.5 degrees so Debbie checked her back into the hospital. She was now in her weakest condition since starting chemo. Cathy said she might have to stay there for five to seven days. She also warned us that there was a high probability that some form of infection would set in. Her mouth sores made it very painful to eat anything. She had a runny nose, she vomited blood, and she had no appetite. She rarely talked and when she did, it was in a hoarse whisper. It helped somewhat to hear from Cathy, Margie, and the rest of the staff that this was the normal reaction, but it tore us up to see our daughter suffer so much.

As strong as Debbie had been, I could tell that deep down she was hurting. I didn't think that Charlotte noticed, but I did. Charlotte lost her first tuft of hair. It just fell out. As medicine improved, I wondered, would we one day look back on this form of treatment as primitive, in the same way we now judged our ancestors for their use of leeches for bleeding and mercury for medicine?

The next day, Charlotte seemed to improve. She asked me to read to her. She got out of bed, walked around the hall a little, and was generally more talkative than she had been for quite some time. Later, Deb – with my moral support – gave Charlotte a combination shower/bath to wash the dead hair off her head. It came off in clumps.

"It's going to take a year and a half to grow back," Debbie said with a deflated sigh.

I nodded. Knowing what to expect still didn't make it easier.

Outside it continued raining, with more rain scheduled through the week. Normally, it never rained so much in the summer. The TV weathermen and everybody else wondered: "What was going on?" Nobody could remember ever having so much rain over such a prolonged period.

At home, Mariella had fun playing with a little plastic flashlight I brought her from the office – a promotional knickknack with some company's logo on it. She called it a "flashing light" and turned it on and off with endless fascination. Mariella, at three, was an interested, inquisitive child. The boys were still babies and content in their playpen.

A normal morning's routine had come to mean Debbie at the hospital while I stayed at home with Mariella, Whitney, and Carter until the sitter arrived and I could leave for the office, with a stop at Mercy to check on Charlotte and Debbie. We felt that Charlotte needed to have one of us with her at all times. The nurses did a wonderful job, but they weren't her parents. And the next time we took Charlotte home, we arranged in home nurses. With four small children, and one of them so ill, the extra help became necessary.

Father's Day brought a welcome reprieve from the rain. It was beautiful outside with a clear blue sky, warm temperature, and low humidity. But Charlotte was back in the hospital with a fever of 102. She also had blood in her urine and vomit. This had the staff concerned. They scheduled her for an endoscopy where a tube would be inserted down her throat for further examination. Charlotte had already lost half of her hair. Once again, she seemed depressed and mad. I shared her disappointment. It seemed like we were tennis balls getting hit back and forth between home and the hospital. And it was a very long rally. Boom, boom, boom, boom. Back and forth. Back and forth. Over and over and over again.

The doctor performing the procedure, an old friend of our family, saw fungal infection inside her stomach, throat, and duodenum. It wasn't a large amount and as usual – it was something to be expected. When the white count dropped so low, the fungus ran wild. Back in the room, Margie stopped by to check on Charlotte.

"The toughest thing isn't the cancer or the chemotherapy, it's the side effects," she said. "It's very tricky managing it all."

"And one thing seems to lead to another," offered Debbie. "The side effects cause side effects."

"You know," I said philosophically, "It's like playing four games of chess at the same time."

"This is no game, Kerrdog."

"Well excuse me, Cruella."

"Cool it," offered Margie. "I don't want to hear you argue. Y'all are too good to be crackin' up on my watch."

Sheepishly, we looked at each other and then down at Charlotte who was still dozing from the anesthesia. Margie tinkered with the IV monitor to make sure it was working properly.

"Okay, Margie. So how long are we in for this time?" asked Debbie.

"Probably 'til next Friday," she answered. "The hospital will not release her until she's been fever free for 48 hours."

Debbie called at 6:00 the following morning to tell me that Charlotte had been vomiting all night. Her hemoglobin count, which monitors the oxygen producing red blood cells, was way down and she needed another blood transfusion. Her fever had finally broken, but Debbie said that I should come down anyway. In addition to the fungal infection, Charlotte had ulcers in her esophagus and duodenum. She was receiving medicine to combat it. This was a critical moment for Charlotte. She and her immune system were very weak. It was awful to see her in such feeble condition. I felt so helpless to do anything.

As her father, I was supposed to protect her and keep her

safe. Her hair was now almost all gone except for a few stub-
born wisps hanging on like the last leaves of a tree in autumn.
She only woke up briefly during the three hours I was there
with Deb and Sally. Cathy Burks confided to us that Charlotte's reaction has been much worse than they anticipated.
Waiting for her to recover was excruciating. I wanted to blame
someone or something for this awfulness.

I closed my eyes for a moment. In my mind, I didn't have
to be there. I saw myself walking away across a hot desert,
a Dali-like landscape where pocket watches folded over bare
tree branches. I looked down below. Way down. Then
I could see them. Time paused so that the cancer demons
might savor every second of the misery they had inflicted. I
stood there looking out her hospital room window. To the
west glared the fiery orb of the afternoon sun. And then I saw
them, fiendish devils amidst a raging inferno, prancing about
but blurred by pillars of smoke that belched from charred
corpses of the eternally damned.

Dirty, dirty bastards. I wanted to squeeze their slimy necks
until their heads exploded. These monsters welcomed an
endless supply of naked sinners flung helplessly into the su-
perheated abyss. Yet the miseries of those cast down to them
grew tiresome. Such wretched souls deserved to be there.
What really convulsed them in hideous shrieks of laughter was
Charlotte's predicament. Those they could torture from way
below Earth's surface meant so much more. The sufferings of
the innocent were exquisite.

Meanwhile, Charlotte continued to vomit and had no interest in food. Neither did I. If she couldn't eat, I didn't want to
either.

Chapter 14: Our Forest

On Sunday morning, Peter DeVeau, the young priest from
Grace and Holy Trinity Cathedral, brought communion to me
at home. Later, I learned that he also took communion to

Debbie at the hospital. It meant a lot that he had come to our home. At the end of every Sunday service, the celebrant always said a blessing for those receiving communion at home or in the hospital. I had always thought of the recipients as elderly or about to die. Good health had made me oblivious to the fact that serious illness can strike anyone. Anytime. Anywhere.

Later that week, Deb and I got to spend an evening together. It was the first time we'd been able to go out together in what seemed like a very long time. We went to a movie and I rediscovered my appetite at the Boulevard Café. The menu featured Mediterranean cuisine like fresh fish and paella. They also had live jazz. We had a chance to catch up and remind ourselves that we were still married. We talked mostly about our children. Deb told me that Charlotte had a new friend named Mika. She and Charlotte were the same age, but Mika had been battling cancer for several years. It seemed like a good idea for her to have a playmate with cancer. Earlier that day, Burks had arranged a consultation to discuss Charlotte's psyche. There were 15 people present ranging from play therapists, nurses, psychologists, volunteers, and social workers. Deb felt really good about it.

We had been told that children who survived cancer usually went on to lead normal lives without any long term psychological damage, but it was still nice that Mercy would go to such lengths to address our child's emotional well being. The concern wasn't so much about her state of mind in the future but right now, while she was undergoing treatment. It was good for her to exhibit anger and feistiness. That meant she would fight harder to survive. The worst thing for her would be withdrawal and depression. So far, the consensus was that Charlotte had held up very well.

It had been unpredictable to see how this ordeal would affect our extended family. We saw quite a range of emotions. My mother had always been an optimist who avoided dwelling on the negative and ugly aspects of life. It was part of her southern sensibility and an effective coping mechanism. Some would call it denial. I figured she was just trying to make the best of a bad situation. It seemed as if my father felt guilty about it. When he looked at Charlotte, a deep sadness came over him. Neither of my parents quite knew how to handle it. They really had not been grandparents that long. It was devastating to realize you were powerless to change certain situations, especially when you had been raised to believe that if you did the right thing, worked hard, and went to church, everything would work out fine. I suspected my parents thought that Charlotte harbored ill feelings towards them because she had said mean things to them or ignored them when they stopped by to visit. I wished they hadn't felt like that. Her illness was not their fault. And deep down Charlotte loved them.

As the days slogged by, Charlotte started feeling better. We really missed her at a family get together at my parent's home in Rockhill. My brother, Edward, cooked a gigantic pot of rigatoni with meatballs. Granddaddy, also known as Whitney Monroe Kerr, and Bea, his new wife, were there along with my other siblings, Mary, Gib, and Bess, and my brother-in-law Joe, Ellie, Reagan, Erin, Mariella, Whitney and Carter. It was warm and relaxed – even with all the little children. Standing out on my parents' driveway we felt the breeze. It picked up in the early evening.

Leafy limbs on every tree bounced and danced. Swaying back and forth, it was like a tree party as the arboreal masses enjoyed each others' company. Yet some leaves fell too soon. Every limb had its early casualties. The old timers would hang on and go out with a blaze of glory in the fall. But even the toughest could only last so long. A tree was like a family with its combination of strong and weak branches. And, like aged trees, old families died to make way for new ones. Nothing on earth lasted forever.

Charlotte's illness had brought us closer as a family. It reminded us that, as awful as it was to go through hardship, Debbie and I were fortunate to have large, close-knit families, a wide circle of friends, and our church, the Cathedral. Experts say that trees standing alone in an open field have a much greater chance of being hit and destroyed by lightning than those grouped together in a grove or forest. That sense of "security in numbers" was also reinforced by having strong connections to a certain place. For us, that place was Kansas City, a town that, for the most part, still retained its character.

In this modern age of hyper mobility, corporate conformity, and overcrowded loneliness, it was good to live in a place where we not only knew we belonged but where we wanted to do so. Here, we were participants, not spectators. Sure, it was easy to unplug and move from city to city. But it took generations to build and maintain roots. And having roots meant that you were a part of something far more lasting than yourself.

Back at Mercy, Debbie and Freeman got along much better. The focus on Charlotte forced us to put aside our differences. We had realized that, deep down, Freeman was a very caring person. How could he practice pediatric oncology and not be that way? And he was passionate about fighting cancer. He despised the disease. I figured that anybody who compared cancer cells to Charlie couldn't be all bad. In Charlotte's next big round of chemo, Freeman planned to lower the dosages and eliminate the drug bleomycin. Charlotte had definitely improved from a week ago. She was smiling and talking like her old self. We felt what we knew was a temporary sense of relief.

It was about 10:00 on a Sunday night. Debbie was at home with the other three children and I was at Mercy to spend the night for a change. Because of the air buildup in her stomach, repeated vomiting, and a fever, she had the gastric tube back in her nose going all the way down to her stomach to siphon the bile. It was irritating and made her thirsty. When she was awake she constantly asked for a drink of water. On top of all this, she had an awful rash of red spots covering her body. Apparently it was a reaction to one of the antibiotics. The next day, the dermatologist visited. In spite of all the discomfort, the little trouper remained in good spirits. She continued to talk away about many different subjects. It seemed like she was trying to make up for lost time over the past couple weeks when she had spoken very little.

"Daddy?"

"Yes, sweetheart."

"What's it like for Gramps in heaven?"

She was referring to Fred Fuller, Debbie's late grandfather on Sally's side of the family.

"Oh, I'm sure he's happy. He and Nanny, your great grandmother, are probably dancing to the music of Glenn Miller. I'll bet he's wearing a tuxedo and she's in a glittering dress."

"What's a tuxedo?"

"That's a real nice outfit that men wear on special occasions."

"And what about Mimi?" Mimi was my late grandmother, Mom's mother. She had been trained as a classical pianist and did several hours of finger exercises daily to the end of her life. We buried her last winter in Little Rock, Arkansas. Charlotte had met her at a family wedding in Greenville, Mississippi.

"What's Mimi doing up in heaven?"

"I'll bet she's playing Mozart on her piano."

"Who's Mozart?"

"Sweetie, Mozart composed some of the greatest music of all time. Today we call it classical music."

"Is he better than Elvis?"

"By far, my dear."

"Dad?"

"Yes."

"How can God take care of Gramps and Mimi up in heaven and still watch out for me down here?"

"Honey, God is very special. He's not only looking out for us, but everybody else in heaven and here on earth. He's very, very powerful."

"Dad?"

"Yes, sweetie."

"What happens when they bury you?"

"Well … Hmm … Let me try to explain … It's … It's sort of like going on a trip to a really nice place - and never coming back home. But when you're there in heaven, you don't get sad about not going back home because heaven is your new home and you know that everyone here will be coming to join you up there. Don't worry, Charlotte. You're not getting buried anytime soon."

Moments later, Charlotte fell asleep and continued deeply snoozing past 8:00 the next morning. Outside a tremendous thunderstorm raged. But Mercy, with its heavy insulation, virtually muffled the sound. The rain came furiously. Debbie brought me a suit and tie so that I could go straight to the office.

That afternoon, Debbie finally brought Charlotte home. When I pulled in the drive, it was just like it used to be a long time ago – before Charlotte took sick. All the children were there to greet me along with Deb, our dog, Punky, and Jamie Ruhl, our wonderful babysitter. Charlotte seemed so happy to be home and feeling well. We watched Mariella play in the sprinkler while Deb held Charlotte who had grown tired from blowing bubbles.

It was also a good day for business. Richard Thompson and Wilhite went under contract on the building in Armourdale. Reluctantly, Wilhite agreed to pay me a commission. Once again, the great paradox of brokerage: They hated you when you couldn't produce a buyer, but they hated it even more when they had to pay you. Closing was set for late August or early September.

This seemed like the first semblance of normal life we've had in almost two months. I tried to soak it all in and store it somewhere as a reserve for the future. We would enjoy this time as we caught our breath and braced ourselves for the next chemo treatment scheduled for July 12th.

We enjoyed a fun-filled weekend. Friday night was the annual 4th of July picnic and fireworks display. Rainy weather and threatening skies kept some people away but the event was still well attended. Jamie took the boys home early, but Charlotte and Mariella stayed to take in the spectacular pyrotechnics. Before the fireworks, the girls had fun catching lightning bugs. Mariella called them "flashing bugs."

Charlotte seemed so much better. Earlier in the evening as we walked across the parking lot into the party, she wore her floppy little striped hat purchased on our Boston trip but when we walked in, she took it off. She was now completely bald but she didn't seem self conscious about it. The fireworks made quite an impression on the girls. Charlotte "oohed" and "aahed" with her friend Emily but Mariella was scared and covered her eyes most of the time.

On Saturday afternoon we went swimming. Charlotte enjoyed jumping to me from the diving board. Later, I picked up barbecue from Gates at 47th and the Paseo right next to Rib Tech - the MIT of Barbecue and it tasted delicious. After dinner we took the girls to see "Snow White." They thoroughly enjoyed it. Mariella grabbed my arm and held on tight during the scary parts. This had been the first "normal" weekend in a long time. We had our family together and made the most of it. It was such a relief to be together and at home with Charlotte on the rebound. It made me realize that I really didn't need very much to be a happy man.

In spite of intermittent sunlight, it was one of the wettest 4th of July weekends on record. At times we felt cooped up when it rained. After the downpour, the temperature shot up into the 90's. With the humidity, it felt like a steam bath. This old river town got sticky in the summertime. It was about to get a lot worse.

Chapter 15: Open Floodgates

And the rain persisted. This summer monsoon had now washed out levees and flooded towns all along the Mississippi and Missouri Rivers. The ground was totally saturated and had no time to dry out before the next rainfall. The flood damage had reached catastrophic proportions for agriculture. Some farmers couldn't harvest their wheat, and many who had planted corn now watched it drown. Others, who didn't plant corn, had no way to plant soybeans. Late crops ran the risk of getting wiped out by an early freeze. The heavy and prolonged rain had a domino effect that could result in a series of crop failures later in the year. The flooding could hurt our overall economy which heavily depended on agribusiness.

Thanks to modern communications, the flooding had so far resulted in minimal loss of life. It was a miracle there hadn't been more human casualties. There was a gruesome occurrence at a cemetery which was inundated. The scouring action of the floodwaters washed out dozens of graves in eastern Missouri. Corpses and coffins were scattered all around Hardin County near St. Louis. They had to be recovered and then reburied. The floods across the region were now a nightly topic on national television.

And the rains continued. July 9th was the longest sustained thunderstorm I could ever remember. Beginning at about midnight the lightning and thunder flashed and bashed nonstop. Repeated lightning bolts brought bone rattling explosions which shook the house. It was so violent that neither Debbie nor I could sleep. Little Mariella didn't like it much either and she climbed into our bed. Through it all, heavy rain cascaded. It finally stopped about 7:00 a.m. when the boys usually woke up.

As it was a lazy Sunday morning, we didn't realize the severity of the flooding until later. Southwest Boulevard was under water due to Turkey Creek, which was once again overwhelmed by runoff from the Kansas side. Indian Creek inundated parts of Overland Park. Brush Creek swamped Ward Parkway and parts of the Plaza, reminding us of the terrible flood in 1977 that killed 26 people and put the entire Plaza under ten feet of water. The Blue River flooded and dumped into the Missouri River, which caused widespread flooding problems all the way to St. Louis. In all, we received five inches of rain on saturated soil. The weather wizards on the local TV stations called for even more rain that night.

That evening I took Charlotte to the hospital for her interferon medicine. She took this in preparation for round two of chemotherapy. At the pool earlier that afternoon, I watched Charlotte and Mariella splash around and marveled at the amount of energy Charlotte had swimming back and forth and all around. She seemed so happy playing with her sister and the other children. But in just a few days, she would be robbed of it once again by another chemo treatment.

The next morning Freeman and Cathy stopped by to see us.

"Good morning, Dr. Freeman, Cathy."

"Good morning, Kerr's," replied Freeman.

"Where's Mom?" asked Cathy.

"We decided to switch things up a little. She needed to see the other children so I brought Charlotte down here last night for her interferon. I guess we're all ready for the next treatment?"

"Not exactly," answered Freeman.

"What's the problem?"

"Yesterday's CT scan picked up two and possibly three cysts

around the pancreas. The cytoxin will sometimes interfere with the ability of the pancreas to produce insulin. I think we should wait a few days for these cysts to dissipate before starting the next treatment."

"Dissipate? You don't think these are new tumors, do you?"

"No. Definitely not. They're just a byproduct of the medicine, the surgery, and the pancreas getting itself back to normal. We should be able to resume treatment in several days."

Cathy spoke up. "It's nothing to worry about. We have to make adjustments in the schedule from time to time. How do you feel, Charlotte?"

"Pretty good," she answered. "Better than most times I'm here."

We all laughed at her response.

"Clever answer, my dear," smiled Freeman. "We'll make you feel better as soon as we can so you can get back home and be with the rest of your family."

As they walked out, Freeman turned to me and said, "Give my best to Debbie."

"Will do, Doctor. Thanks."

Strange as it seemed, I didn't remember a time when Charlotte seemed happier or sweeter. A couple days later, Freeman decided that she could start her second chemo treatment. She was getting cytoxin and handling it really well. She still had a tough time taking the vancomycin paste and troche which help prevent mouth sores. When she came home, she remained in good spirits. She had no hair on her head and had to stay hooked up to the portable IV, but she kept a smile on her face.

When we first discovered Charlotte's illness, I remembered hoping for the day that Charlotte and the rest of us would have adjusted to living with the disease and accepted the treatment as another normal part of our daily lives. I believed we had reached that point. Charlotte's cancer regimen had become almost routine and predictable. One day I changed her Hickman bandage while watching a baseball game on TV. What was once shocking and wrenching has morphed into a regular way of life. A week after her second treatment, Charlotte was neutropenic, which meant her white cell count was low, but she remained happy and active.

Meanwhile, damages from the flooding continued to mount. Mayor Cleaver, the Governor, and other assorted politicians scurried about to inspect the destruction and call press conferences. They solemnly pledged support for flood victims and scored big public relations points, but they offered no relief from the headaches caused by bureaucratic red tape. Business owners felt frustration that they couldn't get back into their buildings until city inspectors certified the soundness of electrical systems. To make matters worse, they couldn't remove debris because law enforcement would not allow trucks into the affected areas.

So far the area hardest hit in Kansas City, Missouri, was Southwest Boulevard. Many businesses there had had it with the frequent flooding and decided to move. Some probably relocated to Kansas. Ironically, much of the floodwater which engulfed the area came from Kansas. To add insult to injury, Johnson County imported most of its water from Kansas City, Missouri, only to return the favor with storm runoff and sewage.

The rains continued with no letup in sight. Flooding seemed to go on everywhere around us. In some Midwestern states, rain fell for twenty days straight, compared to the usual July average of eight to nine days total. More than 50,000 homes were damaged or destroyed along the Mississippi, Missouri, and Illinois Rivers. Des Moines, Iowa, was without potable drinking water for an entire month. Fifty deaths in nine states were attributed to the floods. Damages eventually approached $15 billion. There was growing concern about disease like typhoid fever. We all wondered how long it would take for the waters to recede. The earth was so saturated that there was no place for the water to go.

Vice President Al Gore said it's as if another Great Lake had formed in the region. The cycle of rain to evaporation and back to rain could not stop itself. The weather had always been an important part of our daily lives in this part of the country because of our connection to the land and agriculture. During those days, the weather was the number one topic of conversation wherever one went – the office, church, a bar, etc. Most of us hadn't seen anything like this in our lifetimes. We worried about those who had been damaged and the long term effects.

All we could do was shake our heads and share rumors. Riverside and Parkville flooded, thanks in part to the Army Corps of Engineers. Back in the 1950s, a series of dams and reservoirs like Glen Elder and Lake Perry were constructed across Kansas for flood control. The rains had been so heavy and the big lakes had become so full that the Corps deemed it necessary to release water in order to save the dams from failure. The result was that the Kaw became a massive wall of water "Goin' to Kansas City" to meet the Missouri. The Kaw pushed into the Missouri so hard that it forced water all the way back north five miles to Riverside, breached I-635 and submerged everything all the way north to Highway 9. Hundreds of businesses were engulfed.

Nobody remembered anything like it since 1951. And back then there wasn't the prolonged rainfall we've had this time. This was supposedly a 500-year occurrence. Many roads were closed in and around the city. Now the big question on everyone's mind was whether or not the levees in town could hold. If they failed, Armourdale, the West Bottoms, and North Kansas City would be under water.

Driving along Front Street was especially creepy because the massive torrent was only a few feet below street level. If I-635 could get breached, why wouldn't Front Street? And it was not just the rain here but also the rainfall from up north in Iowa and the Dakotas. I'd never seen the river so high. It was now edging up against the tops of the levees.

Chapter 16: Relief or Disaster

I had just pulled into the parking lot of the Hereford House to meet a prospect for lunch when my phone rang. It was Debbie. She was panicked. Charlotte had accidentally locked herself and the boys in our bedroom. Deb had tried unsuccessfully to talk her through how to unlock the door but it wasn't working.

"I need you, Kerrdog," she pressed.

"I'm on my way, honey. Don't worry."

I hurried into the restaurant to tell Richard Moore why I had to run home. He represented a group interested in buying some of our parking lot properties listed with us by the RTC.

"Why don't I come along?" he responded. "We can talk business on the way."

"That's fine. Let's go."

When we got to the house it was pandemonium. We were unable to get inside the bedroom so I went next door and borrowed the neighbor's ladder. By getting Charlotte to unlock the window and taking the storm window apart from the outside, I was able to gain entry and save the day. Richard held the ladder and then refastened the storm from atop the ladder as I reinserted the screen. With the hot humid weather and my dark slacks I was a sweaty mess but that's part of parenthood. I then insisted on buying Richard's lunch. I hoped we could make the sale but whatever happened, we would still chuckle over our extended lunch meeting for years to come.

The protracted rainstorms really hit home July 20th. Sandbag crews were out in force along the Kaw and Missouri Rivers. National Guardsmen had sealed off access to Armourdale and the West Bottoms. From Case Park on Quality Hill I scanned

those areas with binoculars. Willhite's building, which Richard
Thompson had under contract, looked very vulnerable. If the
levees failed and Armourdale flooded, the property would be
awash and Richard would have no choice but to terminate the
contract to buy the building. That would be very painful to
us financially. I looked around and saw hundreds of people
who had come here to look out upon on the huge, menacing dominatrix of water at the confluence of the Kaw and the
Missouri rivers.

There was nothing we could do to stop her. Below us the
streets of the West Bottoms sat eerily deserted and ready for
whatever punishment she planned to deliver. I wondered
what it must have looked like down there 42 years ago when
she rose up past the second story of the old brick buildings
and the bloated corpses of hogs and cattle bounced around
like corks, never to grace a dinner table.

An old timer standing next to me struck up a conversation.

"I sure hope this don't turn out like the flood of '51."

I lowered the binoculars and glanced over at him.

"Were you here back then?"

"Here? Hell, son, I was down there," he pointed. "It was the
God damnedest mess you ever seen. I worked the stockyards.
They was dead animals ever'where."

"How'd you get around," I asked.

"Had us a motor boat. We was lookin' to rescue anybody
got stranded. Damn water was up twenty foot high on some
'a them buildings. I shined my flashlight inside 'em. I'll never
forget. It was pitch black 'cept for hunnerds a pairs a beady little eyeballs comin' from the window ledges. They was rats."

Out of respect, I grimaced and looked back into the binoculars.

"Did you ever find any people?"

"Oh, yeah. We found a few. But they was already dead. It all
happened too fast. Poor sum bitches never had a chance."

The river finally crested the evening of July 27th and neither breached nor topped the levees. If they could hold on just a little longer under the continued pressure and if the rains would stop, we should be through the worst of it. The Paseo District had been restricted because of street collapses. Taney and Quebec Avenues swallowed whole trucks. But Richard Thompson's building in Armourdale was still dry. While it was too early to assess the damage, I didn't think I'd ever quite look at properties in Riverside the same way – despite the experts who claimed it was an event that shouldn't happen again for another 500 years.

Late in the afternoon, I decided to make a stop at the Zoo Bar at 12th and McGee. It seemed fitting to celebrate that Armourdale and Thompson's pending purchase had so far avoided the river's wrath. Besides, several of my contacts at Interstate Brands Corporation liked to stop in regularly. Why not kill two birds with one stone? It wouldn't be the first time a visit there in an evening led to a new assignment the next day. Interstate, one of the largest bakeries in the United States with brands like Twinkies and Hostess Cupcakes, owned hundreds of properties all over the country. They were constantly buying and selling real estate.

The Zoo was an aptly named dive on the east side of the Downtown Loop. It was a hideout for a variety of hard living types. At any given time, the Zoo contained lawyers, bondsmen, ex-convicts, pro wrestlers, judges, pawn brokers, street bums, private investigators, news reporters, cops, you name it. The place had a gritty feel with graffiti-colored walls and grungy carpet. The faded pictures and dusty knickknacks behind the bar at one time meant something but were now just curiosities. They suggested that the best times were behind us and we might as well drink up because the world, like the river, relentlessly wore away at us and everything we held dear.

It was owned by a lawyer, Preston Cain, who made his living representing assorted miscreants. Several years ago I sold

Preston the building. After he bought it he moved his law offices upstairs and enjoyed the synergistic effects of co-mingling
the clients of his law firm with the patrons of the Zoo. In
many instances, I think they've become one and the same.
Preston was a large man with a misanthropic attitude forged
from years of dealing with hard luck clients.

"Good evening, Sir Charles," I greeted Charlie Erickson, one
of my Interstate contacts. "How about a drink to celebrate?
The levees held!"

"Why thank you, Mr. Kerr," said Charlie. "That's an excellent
idea!"

Charlie was an in-house attorney at Interstate Brands and he
handled real estate. He had been very good to me. We first
met when I cold called him back in 1986. That call resulted in
a sale listing on the old Butternut Bread bakery. By selling it a
few months later, I earned his trust, got some repeat business,
and made a new friend. I would always have a warm spot
for Charlie because I used a portion of that first commission to
buy Debbie's engagement ring.

We traded a few ribald stories and I laughed hysterically at a
joke I would not remember the next day. I bought a couple
of more rounds. The initial bite of the scotch gave way to a
pleasant warmth. Black and white edges of the day took on
a grayish fuzziness. The level of laughter grew louder and the
smoke billowed. Frank Sinatra serenaded us from the jukebox
in the back. I looked at my watch. Damn. Almost 7:00. If I
had one more, that would put me home by 8:00. Very respect-
able by present company standards, but that was comparing
yourself to the worst. Some of these regulars bragged about
going on two day benders. They laughed about how mad
it used to make their wives before they got divorced. Eight
o'clock was borderline bad to Debbie but she didn't get too
upset when I was with the guys from Interstate. After all, it
was business development, right?

As I walked out everybody yelled goodnight and reminded

me to have fun with the kids. The ride home was a blur as I floated along comfortably with the music of Chet Atkins for company. It all came to an abrupt end when I walked through the door. Debbie was scowling, the children were crying, and the house was a mess.

Chapter 17: Our Time

As we neared the end of July, the Great Flood of 1993 left lingering effects. The parking lot at Front Business Center, one of our leasing and management accounts, was impassable by car and the standing water turned the asphalt to mush. We couldn't do anything until the water receded. But there was nowhere for it to go with the river still high and the ground saturated.

The river levels were slowly dropping and now we faced the task of cleaning up an incredible mess. The foul-smelling muck blanketed everything as the waters began to retreat. O'Rourke was so discouraged. His new location in Riverside had ten feet of water over the floor which was itself four feet above ground level. He and his brother, Kevin, faced having to empty the place and squeegee 25,000 square feet of warehouse space covered in putrid slime. We had only negotiated his lease that April. They were just starting to hit their stride after the disruption of moving.

I looked across the giant pools of scum-crusted water in the parking lot. From the northeast I could see the reflection of our downtown skyline in those puddles, and I was reminded that our city also suffered from stagnation. The infrastructure crumbled, the KC School District had imploded, businesses moved out to new suburban locations, and crime had increased. The grime and decay wasn't there 30 or 40 years ago. It all looked so clean and ordered back then – even in the old black and white photos.

Our vacation from Four North drew to a close as Charlotte

prepared to begin her third treatment. She seemed so healthy and happy. Debbie and I hoped her good spirits would survive the next round of chemo. One evening we drove out to the airport to pick up my brother, Gib, who was recently divorced and returning home with his two daughters, Reagan and Erin, for a two-week visit. His ex-wife had him travel to Virginia and back for the scheduled visits – she wouldn't bring them to him. Charlotte and Mariella were so excited to see their cousins. On the way back from the airport, Charlotte rode with Reagan and Erin in my mother's car while Mariella rode with me – which was not to her liking. She probably felt that Charlotte always had her way. Mariella had missed out on a lot with Charlotte's cancer. Charlotte got most of the attention.

We arrived back at Gib's house before the others. Mariella and I had a chance to sit on the steps of the front porch, just the two of us. She marveled at the lightning bugs – "flashing bugs" as she liked to call them – blinking all around Gib's front yard. Normally she would chase after them and catch as many as she could, but she was happy just sitting with me and watching them blink in the darkness. Not many four-year-olds could sit still like this, but Mariella did. We talked without speaking. She had an unusual ability to soak up her surroundings. The air was thick and humid with not a trace of breeze. It was quiet except for the chirping of crickets and the occasional barking of a dog. The annual wail of cicadas was just days away.

Streetlights, shrouded by large shade trees, poured their beams of light onto a small area of the pavement below. Beyond the spot-lit areas were the hidden characters of other households, tucked away at day's end. And inside, each family had its moments of sadness and joy. Life and death. Rich memories that gradually faded into oblivion.

It all passed so quickly. In an instant Mariella would be a grown woman, as if each tiny flash of a lightning bug equaled the true impact that any of us could ever have on this vast universe. I looked out across the yard and registered each blinking light as one more lifetime with my precious daughter. And that's how it was one typical summer evening in Kansas City. Peaceful, mysterious, and, for a moment, timeless.

Charlotte, well into the third treatment, was not as bad as we had anticipated. She had had some nausea and weakness of appetite, but at the same time, she remained active playing with her cousins, Regan and Erin. She rode her bicycle, caught butterflies, and went swimming. She had a few bad moments, but we had seen her much worse.

Yet the week of August 9th, which began so well, rapidly deteriorated. Aunt Charlotte Arrowsmith, for whom Charlotte was named, passed away. We called her "Shaw." She was a no-nonsense type of lady but had a big heart. I first met her on one of my early dates with Debbie when she happened to be in town visiting Rick and Sally. Her wisdom and special intuition led her to predict our engagement. She was a long-time widow and the sister of Debbie's grandfather, Fred Fuller. Though frail and soft spoken, she had a wonderful spirit. At 5:00 p.m. every day she enjoyed a bourbon highball or two, depending on the quality of the present company. Auntie Shaw loved Debbie and we both felt the same way towards her. She was very kind to my brother, Gib, welcoming him into her home on his frequent trips to visit or pick up Reagan and Erin in Charlottesville, Virginia. Her hospitality helped control Gib's travel costs when he really needed it. May she rest in peace.

That same week, Charlotte was back in the hospital and Jamie Ruhl, our babysitter from heaven, left us and moved to Montana. To make matters worse, business limped along at a pace that didn't cover the bills. I felt like the world was imploding one day when I stopped by Four North to check on Charlotte. Debbie was there along with my mother. Charlotte was sleeping. It felt stuffy and cramped in the hospital room.

"How's business?" asked Mom cheerfully.

"Terrible. I can't close a damn thing. People say one thing then do another. On the deals I have done, I can't get paid. Put Charlotte in the mix and I don't know how much more I can take."

My answer caught Debbie off guard. She'd been so focused on Charlotte that she hadn't really thought about my state of mind, not to mention hers.

"Babe, don't get discouraged. That's the worst thing you can do. We all need to hang in right now."

"Over the years your father has had lots of difficult times," Mom chimed in. "Everything always seems to work out in the end. Dad would come home so upset about this or that deal. Three days later I'd ask him what happened and he'd tell me that everything was back on track."

"It gets old having to pull a rabbit out of the hat just to get by," I answered. "I'll figure it out somehow but right now I've got a bad case of the shorts and I'm staring at a huge pile of bills."

"Well, pay them when you can and don't fret about it," said Debbie with a tone of impatience. "Don't you think we have enough to worry about?"

"Look, I'm just frustrated. I can't really do anything to cure Charlotte. On top of that I'm not making enough money. A man is supposed to take care of his family. I need some air."

I walked out to go have a smoke downstairs. On my way, I saw a few of Charlotte's fellow patients in those little red wagons riding around the corridors connected to their IV tubes – smiling and laughing.

"What a jerk," I thought to myself. "Quit feeling sorry for yourself."

It looked like another empty August weekend. Debbie was at the hospital and I was home with the boys. Mariella set off with my parents to the Missouri State Fair in Sedalia and then on to Arrow Rock along with Reagan, Erin, and Gib. I knew she would have fun going through the livestock exhibits and the Missouri Conservation Department's display of wild animals. I wished I could be there as she focused her intense gaze on the creatures in front of her. Pigs, cows, turkeys, otters, coyotes … it didn't matter. Their movements and shapes were so fascinating. But in her mind I knew it was the eyes that sealed the connection. Eyes were the linkage. When she looked into their eyes, she saw her soul mates, fellow travelers in this wonderful adventure of life.

Earlier that day, Charlotte had a seizure that the doctors couldn't explain. The normal causes didn't seem to apply. It happened at about 4:30 in the afternoon. She went rigid and her eyes rolled back into her head. It was frightening for Debbie and Charlotte. The next day, Charlotte got a CT scan of her brain and some other tests in order to figure out the cause. Debbie and I felt that we were overdue for a little good news. The situation with Charlotte was an ongoing challenge, but everything had been going badly. Floods. The real estate recession. When would it stop?

Chapter 18: Summer's End

As August came to a close, Charlotte completed her third chemo treatment and returned home from the hospital. We never learned what caused Charlotte's seizure, but it hadn't recurred. The weather was beautiful with dry, clear blue skies and a high temperature of only 75 degrees, unusually low for the time of year. The cicadas serenaded us with their high pitched buzzing. It was a familiar sound of late summer that came from these ugly looking bugs that spent seven years underground, slowly emerged from the soil to crawl up trees and walls, and then broke out of their shells and flew into the trees where they occupied the rest of their days singing to us. They were the major part of an ecosystem that supported the fearsome looking cicada killer. The cicada killer was a large hornet-like insect with a black abdomen marked by yellow rings. These predators dug nests down into the dirt from which they hunted the cicadas. They paralyzed them with the venom from their stingers and then dragged them to an underground chamber of horrors. Growing up I learned to have no fear of the cicada killers because they would not sting people. We just knew to leave them alone.

That week, two sales closed. How quickly things could turn in the real estate business. One day things were gloomy and the next it was dreamland. And it wasn't just real estate deals which had a way of recovering. It was something far more important – Charlotte.

This was the season of fresh fruit and vegetables. Tomatoes and sweet corn were two of my favorites, especially tomatoes. All at once they were everywhere. People brought them to the office, the grocer had them, and roadside stands sold piles of these homegrown treats ranging from candy-like cherry tomatoes to the giant beefsteak strain which could barely fit in your hand. With all the rain we've had, the tomato crop looked excellent and we would enjoy them through September. We have many ways to enjoy them – sliced with sandwiches and hamburgers, or with mozzarella, basil and vinaigrette dressing, as bruschetta, or broiled with a crust of crumbled crackers.

Labor Day weekend I planned to observe the dove opener with Gib and one of the other brokers in our office, Greg Walker. Hunting spots near a cut wheat field with proximity to water, a gravel road, and a timbered roosting area usually guaranteed some action. Fresh dove was a real treat. The best preparation was what we called a "dove popper." To make these we took a dove breast and separated the meat from the bone. Each breast would yield a couple of pieces of meat about as big around as a silver dollar and a half an inch thick. The meat was dark and very rich, probably full of iron. We'd put a dollop of cream cheese on one piece, add a slice of jalapeno, and sandwich the other piece on top. Then we wrapped it with a strip of bacon and secured it all with a toothpick. After that, we sprinkled it with pepper and carefully gave it a splash of Worcestershire sauce. We cooked them on a hot charcoal grill like a steak. People asked if the cream cheese would melt all over the place but for some reason, it didn't. If you wanted, you could slather them with a little barbeque sauce at the end of the cooking cycle, but they were delicious either way.

One evening, the boys were asleep for the night and I was watching Monday Night Football in the den. The house was quiet and peaceful as Debbie, Charlotte, and Mariella had all left to be with Rick and Sally in Hilton Head, South Carolina. I stayed home with Whitney and Carter. It would have been fun to see Mariella's reaction to the beach and the ocean. Debbie said the girls were having a blast – especially Mariella as she was totally fearless. I wished I could be with her but I was happy she could have the experience.

My favorite time of the year was fast approaching. As the summer came to a close, the air was a little cooler, and I dreamed ahead to days in the field chasing after quail and pheasant. And those powerful, mysterious forces of nature would soon trigger the annual waterfowl migrations from the north. This was the time to squeeze out every drop of living because afterwards, our world went to sleep.

Chapter 19: Death of a Friend

By September, the spiteful harridan of flooding and destruction lay behind us. The river slept, yet signs of her fury were still with us. Driving across the Kaw River on the James Street Bridge one day, I noticed a car partially submerged along the bank. Was it abandoned or were the remains of some poor soul, swept away by floodwaters, still trapped inside? It was more than a reminder of what could happen when the river rose. It was a warning:

"Don't forget me. I will return. And when I do, I will with a merciless vengeance because you irritate me. I only tolerate you stupid little creatures. I could wipe you away like boots mashing an anthill. You think you can make me wait another 500 years before I do it again? Imbeciles! I could do it again next month if I wanted. I'm going to bed now. Do not disturb me."

The boys were growing up quickly. Carter looked at me with his serious brown eyes. Although he was not yet on his feet, Whitney maneuvered around just fine on his hands and knees – always with a big smile on his face. He was such a happy child. Together, these two were everywhere and into everything. We had done our best to "child proof" the house and that was a good thing. The boys seemed much more active than the girls had been at that age.

They got a little stronger every day. Carter stood up calmly holding on to furniture, not fearfully as he had done when he first gained his feet just weeks prior. Whitney started standing just days after Carter. I saw a lot of myself in Carter. He looked like he would have my physique. Whitney would be taller and not as stocky. It was a trade off – one got my looks and the other got my name.

When Deb and the girls returned that Saturday, I picked them up at the airport. It was a memorable Saturday afternoon. I had finished my obligatory yard work and spent the better part of the afternoon with the boys on the patio. There was no better place on earth than Kansas City in the early fall. We savored it. As I alternated holding Whitney and Carter and rocking in the chair, I felt contented and happy.

Prior to picking up Deb and the girls I had fired up the smoker so that we could have ribs for dinner. They might have been my best ever – smoky and tender, with the meat falling off the bone. They were the perfect accompaniment to having the women in my life safely back home. We caught the last of the monarch butterflies from the butterfly bush in the front yard. This bush got its name because it had always attracted butterflies. Charlotte opted to let hers go but Mariella, ever the curious and fascinated nature girl, examined her monarch until it expired. The migration of the monarchs had pretty much worked its way through our part of the country. They always passed through our region in early September. It boggled my mind that these delicate creatures made such a long journey each year. They went from Canada to Central America and then back to Canada every year.

After dropping Charlotte and Mariella at pre-school the next morning, we received bad news. Mika, Charlotte's friend and fellow patient, had passed away at breakfast. That sweet child never really had a chance. Diagnosed with cancer at only 16 months old, she had already endured three separate courses of chemotherapy. Each time the cancer returned. Her parents finally said enough to the suffering. The oncology staff had no more options. She had taken all the chemo her little body could stand. It was a terminal situation.

Mika was only five years old. She was a beautiful little angel who touched everybody around her. As a seasoned veteran of the chemo, she befriended Charlotte. All of the nurses on Four North loved her. Her death hit them hard. They were all in tears. They had tended to her for more than three years and had grown to love her. The day before her death, she had been very active, playing with the other children at the hospital. She was unaware that her caregivers had emptied the arsenal. Suddenly, her breathing became labored and painful. Overnight her condition deteriorated.

It came fast at daylight as Mika told her mother, "I'm going to follow the golden path to heaven, Mommy."

Then she died.

We didn't tell Charlotte.

Chapter 20: Harvest

Charlotte tolerated the fourth chemo treatment very well.

Her appetite remained strong and her spirits were high. She had adjusted to this new way of life. She was much better about accepting the inconvenience and difficulty. On the other hand, Mariella struggled with the lack of attention. It was as if she had reached her limit. At times she was very difficult. When she decided to throw a fit, she became almost uncontrollable. She was one feisty and sassy little girl. Like the deranged newsman from the movie "Network," she was mad as hell and wasn't gonna take it anymore.

And Fall had definitely arrived. The leaves were beginning to change colors. The temperature was cooler. At night, the mercury dropped into the forties. I felt a buzz of excitement in anticipation of another hunting season. I imagined myself treading slowly, a dog frozen on point, knowing that any second a covey would explode in flight. Or I'm crouching in a duck blind as mallards circle overhead; I can hear the whistle of their wings each time they pass, the trained lab next to me trembling with excitement. In the mornings there would be hot coffee and the crunch of frozen grass beneath my boots. I loved the camaraderie of my hunting partners.

October greeted us with a stretch of classic fall weather. On particularly nice days, we called it a "Field and Stream" day in honor of the famous outdoors magazine. The temperature was cool and many of the trees had turned red and yellow. The variety of the colors always cheered me. I also liked the ways a particular tree, especially the maple, would gradually change from partially red to totally crimson in a matter of days, with each day's coloring different from the preceding one.

Their color was extra bright that year. Perhaps it was nature's way of apologizing for all the rain and flooding we had endured over the summer. The scientific explanation was that the more water the roots soaked up, the more sap there was to fill the leaves when they died. More sap equaled more color. The timing was perfect to be in Arrow Rock for the annual Crafts Festival, so we planned a nice three day weekend to hunt dove, fish, check out the harvesting, and relax. I couldn't wait.

The Crafts Festival was a lively time in Arrow Rock. Some years it was a celebration of the harvest. That was one of those really good years when most of the farmers had finished combining the corn and beans. In spite of the floods, this part of Saline County did very well. Because there were so many bottom land areas that lost crops, the farmers in our area expected to see good prices. They were in the mood to cut loose.

One night we went to a barn dance just outside of town. The pasture area around the old barn was full of pickup trucks. Sounds of laughter and the hickory smoke of barbeque greeted us as we walked in. They were roasting pigs on heavy iron spits over a large fire. A country music band entertained the crowd with a lively fiddler and a wailing steel guitar. But best of all, a classic Harvest moon – as orange as a pumpkin – hung low in the sky. Most of the time the farmers were serious and focused on their work in the field, but that night was different. It was one of those years when everything had just flat fallen into place for those who farmed the high ground around Arrow Rock.

I spotted our farmer, Hershel Roth. The previous day we had met him and his crew in the field. They were harvesting the last of the corn. We took turns climbing up the ladder to ride along in the cab of his John Deere combine. It was a huge piece of machinery – a mechanical Mastodon. Mariella and Charlotte loved it. I could tell Hershel liked it too. It made him feel good to do something nice for this bald-headed little girl. Sweeping through the yellowed stalks we saw deer, coyotes, rabbits, and quail flee for their lives. Was this really an example of man against nature? Not hardly. If Hershel hadn't planted the corn, those critters would've been elsewhere. Besides, the harvest left a lot of food to help them survive winter.

By the edge of the timber the deer had stripped clean eight rows of corn. The deer population had exploded in recent years thanks to certain conservation practices by the state of Missouri. But in some respects the efforts were too successful. The deer had become a nuisance. When city folk thought deer, they saw Bambi. When farmers like Hershel pictured deer, they saw thieves.

"Hey Hershel. How the hell are ya?"

"Hello Junior. I'm feelin' great. Got no goddamn complaints."

I could tell from the size of his plastic cup that the world's problems were a distant concern.

"Whatcha drinkin' there?"

"Hershel's gullet wash, young man. Canadian Mist and Mountain Dew. You want you one?"

"Damn. That's sounds awful good. Don't mind if I do."

With that he grabbed another big cup, reached back into the cooler on the gate of his pickup, and swooped up a load of ice. He then proceeded to pour half liquor and half mixer into the cup.

"Here ya go, pardner."

"Mighty nice of ya, Hershel."

I took a gulp.

"Wow! That's awful good. Thanks."

He laughed a deep laugh and leaned back on the gate of the truck.

"You're welcome, Junior. Didn't realize us farm folk knew how to have fun, did ya?"

"You do this every year? It's a helluva party."

"Only when we get it all in. Lots a times it's still settin' out there to dry. This year it worked out. I started shellin' corn a week ago and now I'm done. Think I'll go to Florida this winter."

"You do that and have yourself a good time."

"I'm already doin' that. Har Har Har."

Hershel had a good laugh. It was deep and German, like the roots he and his ancestors had to the land throughout the Midwest. Many of the farmers across the Great Plains had German ancestry. That characteristic discipline continued to run through their bloodlines. I saw it in his sons Kevin and Curtis. They worked hard and got things done. They were self reliant. When something broke, they fixed it. They didn't call a repairman. They made us city folk look so helpless. If the world ever came to an end, the last ones living would be farmers.

To top off the weekend Charlotte caught a largemouth bass about two pounds in size. The smile on her face made me feel like a good father. To bring her happiness was very important. Even when it was something as simple as catching a fish, it helped to offset some of our recent disappointments. Little triumphs invigorated the soul.

Or so I thought, in an uptight, high-minded way. Tut, tut, tut … What really brought joy to Charlotte and Mariella wasn't the fish but the laughter induced by that cheap tribute to flatulence, the "Whoopie Cushion." In a weak moment, I showed them how it worked and they squealed with laughter for hours, blowing it up and sitting on it or thinking they had snuck it on one of the grownups' chairs. After it erupted, the feigned embarrassment of their grandfather was wildly hilarious. Laughter would always beat a smile.

Chapter 21: South Dakota

Charlotte was back in the hospital to receive her fifth treatment on October 12th. Dr. Freeman warned us that this would be a rougher treatment even though he planned to reduce the dosages. He didn't want to put Charlotte at risk with another treatment like the last one. She had seemed to tolerate it pretty well at first but the recovery was rough, and even though her spirits were good, it made her noticeably weaker. What's more, Cathy Burks had dropped hints that we might finish the chemo treatments in December because her white count – the barometer of her immune system – was progressively dropping to dangerous levels.

The day after Charlotte entered the hospital, I joined a dozen of my pals for our much-anticipated annual pheasant hunting trip. We were headed for South Dakota, where the ringnecks were thick, whiskey flowed, and the World Series was on TV. We would play cards, smoke cigars, trade insults, and laugh the whole damn time.

My hunting crew had become a great group of friends. They knew what I'd been going through with Charlotte's illness, but they didn't make a big deal about it. In their own quiet way they'd done things to try to help me out. Ed introduced me to Ronnie Deffenbaugh who controlled the trash business in Kansas City. Deffenbaugh had real estate needs that came up from time to time. I already had two transactions in process with him. And Keith set me up with John Walden, a prominent local food broker. Walden wasn't anywhere near as wealthy as Deffenbaugh but he was a real estate broker's dream. He changed his car, home, girlfriend, and office location on an annual basis.

In spite of its desolate landscape, South Dakota held an impressive variety of wildlife. There were mule deer, reservoirs full of walleye and trout, waterfowl, grouse, sandhill cranes, and Hungarian partridge. But pheasant ruled as the main draw, attracting thousands of hunters from all over the country – even outside the United States. It was the ultimate destination pheasant hunting. It had become a huge part of South Dakota's economy, yet we could go all day without seeing another group of hunters. It was big, open country. At times you could see for miles in several directions.

We stayed at a place just north of Dallas, South Dakota, called "P and R Hunting Lodge" run by Pat and Ruth Taggart and their extended family. It was nothing fancy. Part of our group stayed in a trailer and the rest bunked in an old farmhouse next door. We took our meals and socialized in a Quonset hut just north of the mobile home. The hut was heated by a huge wood-burning stove. Apparently it had rained buckets before our arrival and then dried out quickly, so the place was dusty as usual. In South Dakota in October, the temperature could range from 20 degrees to 80. This trip called for clear skies with mornings in the low 30's and afternoon highs in the low 50's – just about perfect.

When we reached the field we separated into two groups known as "walkers" and "blockers." The walkers fanned out and noisily tromped through the corn toward the blockers stationed at the other end. The walkers, accompanied by the dogs, would flush the pheasant or push them to the blockers whose presence helped contain the birds until the very end when both groups converged and the remaining birds burst into the air, making a desperate attempt at escape. Except for the flankers who would move up 50 to 100 yards out in front, the walkers would stay in a straight line. This prevented the birds from escaping but it also prevented the walkers from shooting each other. The distance of each field was usually a half mile to one mile. It was important for the walkers to move slowly. If they went too fast they would walk over birds only to see them fly off from behind and out of range. It was also important that the line stopped to wait for individuals to collect downed birds. Stopping also had a funny way of making the tight holding birds nervous, which would make them flush.

The blockers patiently waited at the other end of the field as the walkers slowly approached, distinct in their blaze orange. Sometimes the wait could be tedious if walkers had trouble finding dead birds. Sometimes bitter cold wind made standing still seem like torture. But it was also fascinating to see a panorama of hunters, dogs, and flushing birds all moving together choreographically. The flushing birds flew right at you – challenging you to take the shot. From a distance of a quarter mile, it was common to see the birds hit and falling from the sky before hearing the report of the shotgun. And sometimes there were a few surprises: giant whitetail and mule deer charging out of the cover with racks as big as rocking chairs. Woe to the poor hunter who got in their way. It would have been like getting hit by a truck. We also saw huge jackrabbits and coyotes.

Tension increased as the walkers drew closer to the blockers and birds started flying in every direction. Some snuck through and others were downed. One large rooster miraculously ran a gauntlet of several hunters shooting at him multiple times. We looked on with amazement as he flew off seemingly unscathed when suddenly his flight pattern changed and he went vertical, climbing higher and higher. He then seized up and dropped to the earth – dead as a stone. Other birds got hit hard and folded up only to bounce back to life when they hit the ground and ran off. These were very tough birds. Sometimes, the shooting was pretty intense for the blockers as the birds came boiling out of the field as we tried to reload with birds flying past. As the two groups got within range of each other, we had to be careful to aim high and to hold off on shooting at low flying birds between us. This point of the hunt was the most dangerous and action-packed.

We only shot the brightly colored roosters. It was illegal to shoot hens. Under certain lighting conditions it was difficult to tell the hens from the roosters. Pity the hapless hunter who shot a hen. He would suffer derision from the group for the rest of the trip.

After the last bird had flown we came together for a few minutes to congratulate each other and get a drink of water. Then we counted up the birds and headed for the next field. Because of all the rain prior to our arrival, most of the grain had not been harvested. As a result, the pheasant were more dispersed and not as bunched up. We had to work harder for our birds but we still got them.

The last day had the best action. After the hunt, we packed up and grabbed a quick lunch before the hour-and-a-half ride to the airport in Mitchell, South Dakota. Mitchell was best known as the home of the Corn Palace, an entertainment venue with its exterior completely covered with intricate designs fashioned entirely from ears of corn. I felt deflated on the drive. The trip I looked forward to so much was over in a flash. It seemed like we had just arrived. I wished I could stay up here longer. The three days wasn't enough. We crossed over the Missouri River. At this point it was very wide. It looked more like a lake than a river. It was bright blue and sparkled in the sun. It was nothing like the brownish mass that oozed its way through Kansas City. Now it was back to reality.

Chapter 22: Still Married – And Happily

A message was waiting for me when I stepped off the jet: Charlotte was back in the hospital. She had suffered some serious side effects from treatment number five. I felt very guilty that I had been gone and drove straight to the hospital. Outside, fall was in its full glory and Charlotte was stuck on Four North. Soon the leaves would shrivel up and turn brown just like the remaining cancer cells inside her body – I hoped. When I reached Four North, I sat on the edge of her bed and ran my hand over her head.

"How's my big girl? I missed you."

"Dad, this cancer makes me mad! I hate it!"

"I know sweetie. But you get to go home tomorrow."

"I want to go home now!"

"We need to make sure it's safe. If we don't, we'll have to turn right around and bring you back. You don't want that to happen, do you? You know that's no fun."

"Daddy," she pleaded. "I want to be at home with you and

Mommy."

"I know sweetie. We want you home too. Just try to be patient."

As disappointed as she would get, Charlotte and her fellow patients found ways to make the best of it. She has taken a special interest in another little patient named Ashley. Ashley was only 13 months old. Charlotte wanted to play with her all the time. And, excited about the approach of Halloween, Charlotte and another patient, Eric, worked an entire afternoon and turned her room at Four North into a haunted house complete with ghosts, skeletons, creepy music, and spider webs. Charlotte and Eric hid in the darkened bathroom with a flashlight ready to jump out and scare those brave enough to venture in. Little Eric had a tough situation on the home front. He was an inner city kid who had to get a cab ride to the hospital for his chemo treatments. He was the same age as Charlotte.

It was difficult for Charlotte and Eric to truly hide, hooked up as they were to their rolling IV trees which were visible and obvious to those who came to visit this scary place. Apparently the nurses, staff, other patients, and parents stopped by all day long to visit Charlotte's haunted house. It was quite a sensation and it did wonders for her spirits. Charlotte just kept improving. It amazed us how she bounced back after each treatment. Although she was fighting a cold, she had a healthy appetite and lots of energy.

Debbie had a much better handle on children like Eric, who mostly spent time on Four North alone. Many nights she comforted children whose parents were away, rocking them to sleep. She usually did it after Charlotte was down for the night but sometimes she'd pull Charlotte along in the red wagon. One of her favorites was an 18-month-old girl whose parents were unable to be there. That child cried every night but Debbie was able to get her asleep. If, at that moment, Raphael could have come back to life and painted the scene of Debbie, Charlotte, and that little girl, he would have named it

"Madonna of Mercy."

It was now official. Charlotte's chemo treatments would end in December. Freeman and his staff believed that she had had enough. Any more chemo beyond December would likely lead to an infection, especially at that time of year when colds and the flu ran rampant. To celebrate, Debbie and I decided to go out to dinner. We went to Michael Forbes Grill in the area of town known as Waldo. The crowd wasn't huge and since we weren't in a hurry we decided to have a couple drinks at the bar before sitting down at a booth.

"Here's to you, Deb, for keeping it together during a tough time," I offered.

"I couldn't do it without you, baby," she smiled as she winked at me over her Dewar's and soda.

"I still look back on all this like it's some kind of a bizarre, never ending dream. But what's weird is I really don't remember much what things were like before Charlotte got sick. It all seems so distant now."

"It's no dream, Babe. But we'll get through it. One day at a time. We have to keep the faith and work together as a team."

She reached over and squeezed my hand.

"They say things like this have ruined a lot of marriages. We need to remember that."

"Amen, sweetheart. What's that old saying? What doesn't kill you makes you stronger. Anyway, I feel really good about where we are, don't you? Life's complicated enough. We couldn't split up even if we wanted to. Couldn't afford it."

I winked and grinned at her.

"Looks like we're stuck with each other. Cheers."

We clinked our glasses together.

"Yes, but we can't take each other for granted, even when things get really bad with Charlotte."

I lit up a smoke and she frowned at me.

"You know I don't like you doing that, Whitney, especially when we have a child with cancer."

"Yeah , yeah….. but you know how I like to smoke when I'm having a drink. Besides, if cancer can strike an innocent four year old, what's the damn point of going through life without a little indulgence here and there? I could deny myself a lot of things for the next few years in hopes of a long life. Then one day I walk out and get splattered by a truck.   And for what?"

She frowned and shook her head.

"I sometimes wonder how I ended up with you. All the good men out there and I married you."

Then she smiled and stuck her tongue out at me.

"My dear, you must never forget how incredibly lucky you were to land a man of my caliber."

"Yeah, right, you pain in the ass!"

"Seriously, though."

She rolled her eyes at me.

"C'mon. I mean it. Do you ever wonder how this will change us? I keep hearing how experiences like this reshape a person."

She was thoughtful for a moment.

"I'm sorta' mixed on that. We're wired to handle a certain amount of adversity. We can't just fall apart the minute things get tough, you know? But there is something I've been feeling lately. Before there was a part of me that was happy go lucky, just humming along and taking it all for granted. I think I've lost some of that."

"Yeah, I know what you mean. I guess it's just a part of getting older. Not much we can do about it. As time goes by our childish wonder for the world fades to a mellow appreciation."

I tipped my cocktail glass and drained it.

"Things are going smoothly and then life suddenly takes a bite out of you. Turns on you like an angry dog."

"Yeah," she laughed. "Like a Kerrdog."

"You know how I feel different?" I asked.

"How's that?"

"I have a new found freedom. Freedom from worrying about what other people think. All my life I've tried to please everybody. I don't give a damn about that anymore. What matters most is taking care of my family. The social stuff just doesn't seem important anymore. Charlotte's cancer has helped me realize that."

"Well, don't be so quick to abandon all that. When our lives get back to normal we may go back to some of those things. Some of that social stuff does good things for the community."

"Yeah, maybe … Maybe so."

Chapter 23: Winter's Threat

The weather turned colder and we began to see snow flurries. I was stoked about the annual quail opener. Joe, Duayne, Ed, and I planned to leave for Arrow Rock after I took the girls trick or treating. Charlotte was back home in time for the "real" Halloween. If it wasn't too windy, the hunting would be good. I had lined up more than 1,100 acres for us to hunt, and we would have good dogs working for us. If we didn't find birds, they just weren't there.

The quail hunt to Arrow Rock was cut short one day due to rain. Monday's hunt netted only a dozen birds. Normally, a group of four hunters at Arrow Rock should bag at least a couple dozen. It wasn't for lack of opportunity. We saw more than ten big coveys but our shooting was atrocious and the birds didn't work quite right. It seemed like they flew into timber on almost every covey rise. There was very little singles action – my favorite part of the hunt. It convinced me that we had a new species in Arrow Rock, the timber quail, a special breed conditioned to fly into the woods on the hunters' approach and never hold a point.

My second favorite part of the hunt was at dusk when the group sat down to unwind with a drink or two after a full day in the field. We had the grill set up for steaks on the patio of the Townsend house. Duayne and I took the quail along with cleaning shears and a scotch down to the back fence. We made quick work of it, first snipping off the heads –white heads were cocks and yellow were hens – then the wings and the feet up to where the feathers started. Next we pinched the skin and feathers in the lower abdominal area. With a firm tug it came loose to reveal the pinkish breast. The true gourmand would probably sniff at our skin removal technique but plucking a quail took too much time. From that point it was simply a matter of tugging the skin and feathers downward from the neck and away from the rest of the body – almost like removing a jacket. As we did this we found the craw sac at each neck full of soybeans, one of their favorite foods this time of year. Next we cut off the tuft of feathers and the lower part of the rump. Then we inserted the shears into either the neck or lower abdominal cavity and cut out the backbone going up one side and down the other. When we lifted the spine away, it pulled out the entrails and presto … a cleaned bird. We tossed each one into a bowl. Later, in the kitchen, we would rinse them off and with our thumbs peel away the remaining parts of lung and kidney which sometimes stuck to the spine. We'd also make sure to dig out pellets and any feathers pushed into the meat by the shot. Feathers didn't taste very well.

After drying my hands with an old towel, I lit a smoke and turned to Duayne, "Well, old man, not such a bad day, was it?"

"Not bad at all! It was a good day, bud. The dogs worked nice and my knee didn't complain too much. Hell, we got into ten coveys."

"Beats the hell outta workin', don't it?"

"Every time. Hey, don't forget - we got duck season comin'. We gotta getchur' ass to Blairstown. Regan and the Linn brothers'll be there. We'll have us a good time. But it's still early yet. Them red legs ain't quite made it down here yet. We need a big cold front to push 'em. All we got now are locals."

"I'm ready anytime. It's hunting season. My favorite time of the year. And Regan's usually good for several hundred bucks at the gin rummy table. I could use the money too."

"These birds'll make a nice appetizer. How you wanna cook 'em?"

"Well, here at Chez Kerr, we have two choices. We can do the standard bacon wrap, garlic clove in the cavity, and toss 'em on the grill with the steaks. Or, we can marinate 'em in teriyaki sauce, wait a while, and then throw 'em on the grill with the steaks. Only problem is, if we go the marinade route, we might have to drink a little longer."

"Hmmmn … Sounds like we better go with the teriyaki."

"How'd you get to be so damn smart?"

It was dark. Suddenly, from the north, came the wailing cries of coyotes. There must have been 20 of them in the pack. They sounded pretty close and their high-pitched howls grew more and more urgent. We'd usually hear it this time of night, just after sunset. But it was more than the sound of coyotes. It was the sound of death.

"Damn," said Duayne. "That's a regular feeding frenzy. Some poor critter is gettin 'et up pretty good."

The high pitched yelps had now reached a fever pitch. The yips and shrieks grew frantic. From the fury of it I couldn't tell predator from prey.

"What'd they be feasting on tonight?" I wondered.

"Oh, could be a stray dog or an injured deer. Whatever it was, is sure one sorry sum' bitch."

"You know, Duayne, all suffering aside – that's what I love about coming down here. It's back to the basics. Coyotes don't need a damn permit to take care of business. Ain't a buncha goofy ass laws and regulations out there in that field right now."

"That's right, bud, nothin' but the laws of nature."

And then, just as suddenly as it had started, it grew quiet. A life had been sacrificed in order to prolong that of others. It was a basic scene of nature that played repeatedly but one which always captured our attention. There was nothing like experiencing it firsthand, the desperate struggle between death and survival – and the reminder that we too have a small role on the same grand stage. Hopefully, we and our loved ones would never perish with such savagery. But Death doesn't care how we get to the final meeting – just that we show up. And his favorite time of the year was rapidly approaching.

Debbie has her hands full!

Aunt Bess with Charlotte and her daughter Ellie.

Whitney, Charlotte, Carter and Mariella at bath time.

South Dakota hunting crew.

**Charlotte and Mariella at Halloween - that's Sally Ramos
in the background.**

Charlotte with Dr. Freeman.

Charlotte and Mariella with their cousins Reagan and Erin (sitting on the stairs).

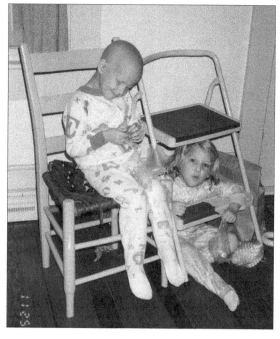

Charlotte and Mariella in Arrow Rock.

Charlotte and Mariella with their grandparents, Whitney and Day Kerr.

Charlotte and Mariella with Snow White.

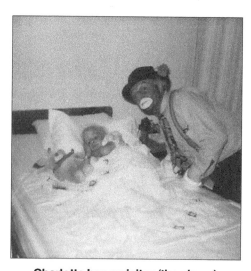

Charlotte has a visitor (the clown).

Children at Christmas.

Charlotte and Mariella sleeping in Mom and Dad's bed.

Disney World.

Her hair is starting to grow back.

Part three:
Survival and Recovery

Chapter 24: Jimmy from Joplin

Charlotte was about to begin yet another treatment. It would be her second to last. She had energy, an appetite, and she was happy. If not for her bald head, I could have thought she'd never been sick. I had almost forgotten what Charlotte looked like with hair until Deb set out some newly developed pictures in the living room. They were pre-chemo pictures from our trip to Boston for the second opinion.

It was another beautiful fall day. Clear blue skies and 50-degree temperature. We had the children outside and it did us all good to breathe the crisp autumn air. We videotaped them playing in piles of leaves. It reminded me of when I was a little boy making leaf forts with my siblings and the other neighborhood children. Back then we piled the leaves by the curb and burned them. It smelled great. It smelled like fall. Now it was against the law because it supposedly polluted the air. In our great wisdom we hauled piles of plastic bags to the landfill and buried them. And that distinctive smell of burning leaves was just a distant memory from simpler days gone by.

What was supposedly a "routine and light" treatment became difficult. Charlotte was exposed to chicken pox in the oncology clinic of all places. She had to receive a vaccination before she could come home after spending one night at the hospital to receive interferon, cisplatin, and others. Because of three relapses and four new cases, Four North was filled to capacity. We had to double up overnight with another family because Charlotte wasn't yet neutropenic.

To make matters worse, Charlotte's urinary output had dropped way off from where it should have been. We'd known all along that the chemo could cause kidney problems. Was Charlotte going to experience kidney failure and succumb to dreaded dialysis? Just when the end of her chemotherapy was in sight?

I could tell that Deb was feeling stressed. The constant attention to Charlotte and the other children had taken its toll. She needed a break. So did Mariella. The little princess had really had a tough go of it. Charlotte was always the center of attention and Mariella got neglected. I worried that someday she might have emotional problems attributable to this period in our lives. Deb and I both felt guilty about not spending enough time with her. This weekend I hoped to take her to the Kansas City Museum and then to lunch at Skies, a revolving restaurant atop the Hyatt Regency Hotel. But now that Charlotte had a fever, nausea, lack of appetite, and poor kidney functions, we had to check her back into the hospital. Mariella and I had to postpone our date.

As a fitting piece de resistance to our anxiety, some punk broke into my car when it was parked on the street in front of our house. He smashed out a window and bent up the door with a crow bar; something not big enough to file a claim on, but worth several 100 dollars and a lot of inconvenience.

In the hospital, Charlotte remained brave but, another fellow cancer patient, little Jimmy Norris from Joplin, passed away. Early on in Charlotte's illness, he was one of her fellow patients who made me realize that I had no right to feel sorry for myself. He was the one who not only had cancer but was also mentally retarded. He never had much of a chance in life. Now he was gone. Most of us would like to think that our lives served some kind of purpose – that we made the world a little better for having been here. In his own way Jimmy accomplished that. I'd thought a lot about Jimmy. He was always smiling, even at times when he must have felt awful. And he shared that happiness with those around him. By doing that, he made the most of what was given him. He proved that every life has meaning. He showed me that most of us expect too much and then feel bad when we don't get all the things we want. He made me realize that we spend too much time striving for more when we ought to be grateful for what we have.

Debbie and I both breathed huge sighs of relief when Charlotte's kidney functions returned to normal. The worries of kidney failure and dialysis were behind us for the time being but she was still very weak. She had been sleeping quite a lot. Once again she appeared to be making a gradual recovery from the latest chemo treatment, but it took her longer to recover from this round.

Chapter 25: A Nice Neighborhood

Charlotte turned five on November 19th, and was feeling well enough to have a festive birthday party. There was a clown, pizza, and lots of commotion from a dozen children, including three from Four North.

That next fall, she would start kindergarten. That fact made me realize we needed to move. Our house in Brookside had become too small for six people. Not to mention the Kansas City, Missouri, public schools – schools I had once attended – no longer offered quality education. Families were leaving the district in droves and reluctantly, I saw that we must follow. As families continued to leave Missouri, massive new residential developments were springing up across State Line. In Johnson County, Kansas, we would have neighborhood schools and quality education.

But the situation gnawed at me. This was the second time that I left the district. The first was 20 years ago when I transferred from Southwest High School to Rockhurst after the teachers of the Kansas City Missouri School District went on strike in 1974. The state line was a curse on Kansas City. It provided an easy way out. Instead of taking a stand and fighting to make things better, all we had to do was pack up and move to Kansas. Not much different from the transients along the Missouri River, leave things a mess and move on to the next campsite.

November 21st was my 35th birthday. Deb kidnapped me that Saturday afternoon. We spent the night at the Allis Plaza and dined at the Savoy. It was a wonderful evening. Deb really did a nice job arranging everything. We sat in the Truman booth. It was the same booth Harry Truman preferred to use back in the '50s after he'd returned from Washington, D.C. The Savoy Grill had always been my favorite restaurant in Kansas City. Back in the kitchen there was a giant lobster tank. The fish were flown in daily from the east coast. The white jacketed waiters were well trained and the service was attentive but low key.

Perhaps it was inevitable but a little boy at Charlotte's preschool made fun of her baldness that day. It really upset her. While there were many byproducts of her illness out of our control, there were some things which we should have the ability to eliminate. Children making fun of her at school was certainly one of those. Charlotte couldn't live her life in a bubble but at the same time she shouldn't get kicked when she's down. It has always been puzzling how seemingly sweet little children could be so mean to each other. I guessed it was in their genes.

The next day we left for Arrow Rock where we planned to celebrate Thanksgiving at the newly renovated Prairie Park. Our gathering at the farm this year was an especially gratifying way to spend the holiday. And, like the pilgrims many years ago, we too had enjoyed a bountiful harvest. When the Roth's harvested the corn and beans in October, the yields were good – 175 bushels per acre on the corn and 50 bushels on the beans. Hershel was an astute farmer. Before he would commit to farm for us, he insisted that Dad have grain bins on site so that we would not be at the mercy of the elevator operators.

The elevators not only charged for storage but they penalized the farmers when the moisture content of the grain was too high. By having our own storage capacity, we not only could dry the grain with blowers set inside the bins but could also wait to sell when we thought the market was right.

We celebrated our first Thanksgiving at Prairie Park in grand style. Present were Granddaddy, Bea, Mom and Dad, Gib, Mary, Bess and Joe and Ellie, Deb and I, Charlotte, Mariella, Whitney, Carter, and Aunt Frances, Granddaddy's sister who never married and recently moved back to Kansas City after an interesting career with the State Department in Washington, D.C. Prairie Park had been restored to its original beauty with decorative plaster, 14-foot ceilings, glittering chandeliers, and original antique furniture. It also figured importantly in the history of Missouri. Two state governors, Meredith Miles Marmaduke and Claiborne Fox Jackson, were buried in the Sappington family cemetery, a state historic site, just down the road to the west. My parents did a remarkable job overseeing the project.

Thursday morning, before the big dinner, Gib, Joe, and I went quail hunting. The conditions seemed ideal – twenty degrees, a little wind, frozen brush – but we didn't see many birds. After about an hour and a half, Duchess, Joe's Brittany, went down on a solid point. Finally sensing some action, we closed in only to see a couple of nice gobblers pop up and fly off. One had a beard at least ten inches. But turkeys were out of season after October, so we held off from shooting. It ought to be legal to shoot a turkey on Thanksgiving.

Our Thanksgiving dinner was very nice but hectic with all the little children. We had a 25-pound turkey, lightly browned and cooked to perfection with dressing, piles of buttered broccoli, steaming bowls of mashed and sweet potatoes, cranberry sauce, celery, olives, carrots, biscuits, baked squash, and pumpkin pie. Dad always insisted on mincemeat pie but he was the only one who ate it. He could have it all to himself as far as the rest of us were concerned. For him, that was another thing to be thankful for: an abundant supply of something nobody else but you wanted.

After we had gathered around the dining room table and said the blessing, Mariella, inspired by the lovely setting and festive mood piped up saying, "This is a very nice neighborhood."

Her timing was perfect and everybody thought it was hilarious, and bless her heart, Mariella was a little taken aback by our reaction. In her mind, she was trying to express appreciation for being part of such a special occasion and she thought we were laughing at her. We reassured her that her comment was most appropriate.

Deb gave her a hug, "Yes, sugar, this is a nice neighborhood. Thank you for noticing."

The next day we helped my parents move an enormous antique piano into one of the parlors. It belonged to the Sappington family who originally built Prairie Park and was now returned to its proper place on loan from the Friends of Arrow Rock.

That afternoon I went out by myself and shot a couple of rabbits. Debbie cooked them in the skillet with onions and mushrooms. They were delicious. We had no television at the Townsend house. For entertainment, we just had our immediate family. We spent the evening around the wood stove reading and playing games with the children. It was almost as if we had stepped back in time, living off the land and enjoying a simpler, more wholesome life.

We returned to Kansas City just as the snowstorm began. The accumulation came to three inches and the girls were thrilled. The long weekend had flown by. The extra time with the children was fun. Charlotte and Mariella helped me pick out a Christmas tree. We set it up in the corner of the living room. It was a pretty tree that had the fresh smell of pine along with rich color and nice proportions. In the morning we went to Lamar's for donuts. We also built a snowman and then threw snowballs when the sun came out.

Charlotte's preschool teacher shared with us that the Reverend Cooney, minister of Country Club Christian Church, addressed the assembled preschoolers prior to Thanksgiving. The purpose of his talk was to remind the children that there were many people less fortunate and that some of them may not be able to afford a nice dinner. At this point in his talk, Charlotte's hand shot up and he called on her.

"Do you have something to share with us, Charlotte?"

"If they don't have enough money, all they need to do is go out and make a big real estate deal."

Charlotte said this with all the sincerity and consideration a five year old could muster. Her comment really caught Reverend Cooney off guard and the other teachers present had to bite their lips to keep from laughing. Yeah. Real simple, I thought. All they had to do was to just go out and make a real estate deal – at a time when even seasoned brokers had a tough time doing it.

Chapter 26: Jamelle

Charlotte went on December 6th for her last chemo treatment. It was not going well. Her blood counts never really came back from the last treatment. It got scary when her immune system was weak at this time of year with everybody sick. She was running a fever, had nausea and diarrhea. Freeman cancelled the last of the interferon because she was feeling so badly. At this point, the chemo was over. Now we would wait for her to recover and then move on to radiation treatments. She had suffered so much. She needed to regain her strength and avoid coming down with a cold.

Outside the temperature had dropped. It'd become very cold and winter had only just started. Deb thought Charlotte might have to stay in for as long as a week. It was disappointing. The girls had been invited by the home healthcare people to attend Disney on Ice. Charlotte, Mariella, Deb, and I were to get front row seats, a special pre-party to meet the characters, and a spin on the ice. It didn't look very likely.

The fall season brought a festival-like atmosphere with the bright colors of changing leaves, brassy marching bands, and frantic broadcasters trying to make themselves heard over the roar of a crowd. Combines rumbled over rows of corn. It was a time of excitement and anticipation. Summer's humidity and sweat gave way to coolness and comfort. More than any other, it was the season of celebration.

But by late December those feelings had disappeared. Most stadiums now sat empty. The duck hunting marshes were frozen solid. The leafless trees now hung like skeletons. It was a somber time when Mother Earth slept. The obituary section of the Kansas City Star ran longer at the end of the year. Some included pictures of the deceased. Most did not. It really didn't matter. Most of us would soon be forgotten.

Winter was the loneliest season. Out the front bay window, above the brownish tree line was the vast emptiness of white sky, gauzy yet impenetrable, a hovering blank canvas. Not even a solitary crow to break things up. It was utterly lifeless. The blankness equaled the sum total of my efforts to crack the code to this perplexing world. I wanted to understand why my five-year-old daughter was fighting for her life. I wanted to figure out how I could make some kind of a lasting impression while I was here. I wanted our lives to be more than the flash of a lightning bug. Maybe I could be an extra bright lightning bug. Some of us were like that. But even then, we were only lightning bugs. And all I could do was draw a blank.

Perhaps that's the way God meant it to be. Twenty-thousand years from now Julius Caesar and George Washington would be blended together in the same tar pit with Charlotte's fellow cancer patients and the rest of us. The important people of our time would be utterly erased in relatively short order. Our stay on Earth was just a part of the journey.

I looked down at the driveway where Charlotte carelessly left her Barbie car so that Debbie or I would run over it with an adult vehicle. Somebody needed to put the Barbie car away. "At least I could understand that," I thought to myself. Let others answer the complicated questions. I was at my limit just trying to take care of my family. The stress of the holidays hit us with a delayed reaction after days of outings, errands, and hauling the children to and fro. Deb and I both felt exhausted.

Then came more bad news from the hospital. The kind of news that made our concerns seem small. Another fellow patient, Jamelle Williams, passed away December 22nd. His funeral was held on Christmas Eve. Debbie attended. His overburdened mother had just given birth to twins. Our similarities to Jamelle's family didn't go unnoticed. Jamelle fought hard but succumbed after his treatments failed and the tumors grew terrifically fast. It was as if his cancer was programmed to destroy him from the beginning, with no chance of survival. Jamelle was gone at the tender age of six, never to experience what we considered a full life. Meanwhile, his family would live on with the permanent emptiness of where he once was. We felt very sad for their loss and hoped that the Williams family could find solace with their new babies.

I wanted to believe that Jamelle did not die in vain. Like Jimmy from Joplin, I told myself that he left the world a better place. Children's Mercy conducted extensive research and the particulars of Jamelle's case, when added to the body of existing knowledge, could someday tip the scales in favor of a cure or a better form of treatment for the strain of cancer that took his life. In his suffering, he may have helped future children.

"Yeah sure," the Williams' might have said. It sounded really wonderful – until it was your child doing the dying.

But things improved. Charlotte felt so much better that Tamara Minks of Children's Home Healthcare took Charlotte,

Mariella, Deb, and me to the Disney on Ice production of "Beauty and the Beast." The big evening we thought we'd have to miss came together after all. It was fantastic. We had front row seats, pictures with the characters, and a stop at the revolving restaurant Skies atop the Hyatt beforehand. The girls were fascinated with the panoramic view of the city. It was a big boost to our spirits as we headed into Christmas.

The girls were growing more and more excited. Charlotte wanted a hamster and Mariella wanted Lego Maniacs. Our tree was fully decorated with ornaments, I'd strung the lights on the house outside, we have had some nice parties, and my entire family would be in town.

On Christmas Eve we took the girls to the early service at the Cathedral in a mild blizzard. We had a white Christmas. Charlotte and Mariella really enjoyed their presents. For them, the real thrill was in opening rather than having them. They tore into each present like a buzz saw, smiled when they recognized what it was, and then quickly set it aside and reached for the next one. Charlotte had a hamster and Mariella had her Lego Maniacs – a very complicated toy to assemble.

Edward was here until after New Year's. Ben and Debbie's sister, Karen, and their daughter, Macy Belle were in from Nashville. Gib's daughters, Reagan and Erin, would arrive the day after Christmas to visit for a couple weeks. It has been hectic trying to spend time with our families and friends. I was not sure how much she really liked it, but Debbie seemed to get us into all kinds of obligations which made the holidays more stressful. I caught myself trying to find ways to simplify the whole experience. I wanted time to relax and reflect but we got so caught up in the trappings of the season that we forgot how to enjoy it.

My parents had a gathering of the Kerr clan at their house. Our schedules had grown so crowded that our annual family get together happened post Christmas. It was probably better this way because after Christmas, people were more relaxed.

It was a big gathering – Granddaddy and Bea, Phyllis, David, Karen and baby Jacqueline, Mary, Edward, Bess, Joe, and Ellie, Gib, Reagan and Erin, and our own group of six. Also, Dad's sister Mary and her husband Bob along with their children Angie, Chip, and Brett. There were 26 people in all and a fun group at that. My grandfather liked to come dressed in his green and red plaid slacks made of the famous Kerr plaid from Scotland. The men in the family had neckties in the same pattern which we also wore, celebrating our heritage just as our Scots-Irish ancestors did for centuries before us – except that at this gathering we'd skip the brawling. We've talked about getting kilts.

All of us were fighting head colds. Charlotte's counts remained low and that concerned us. We hoped to learn in January the next course of treatment. On the one hand, we believed we were on the road to recovery and that the worst was behind us. Yet, with the ongoing monitoring, we would not be done with this for years and we had to get used to living with the possibility that she could relapse. The rule of thumb was that you're not in the clear until five years after completing treatment. That meant we would be under a cloud of uncertainty until 1999.

It was now 1994. The New Year had arrived and we looked forward to it with extra anticipation because the difficulties of 1993 were finally behind us. Charlotte had finished chemo and we hoped for the return of a normal, healthy lifestyle. Everything would improve this year, especially Charlotte.

Chapter 27: Abandoned Farmhouse

On January 9th at 5:00 a.m. I arrived at Hayo's to go pheasant hunting. Along with Tony, Donnie, and Tom, we planned to hunt around Hiawatha, Norton, and Sabetha in northeastern Kansas. Unlike many of my previous bird hunts that year, the action was nonstop. It was very cold at 20 degrees with brisk winds, which gave us a wind chill at times close to zero. We did find birds. All day long we got into a mix of quail and pheasant. Mike's two Brittany spaniels were regularly on point as we worked a combination of fence rows, cut milo, and brushy draws. We found most of the birds in low spots down out of the wind.

Late in the morning we took a break at an old abandoned farmhouse. Hundreds of these relics, like prairie shipwrecks, dotted the Kansas landscape. Each had a story about the people who once lived there. This one looked like it had been built in the last quarter of the 19th century when westward expansion was booming. At one time it had been a nice home with plastered walls, a second floor, and multiple rooms. But decades of neglect had taken a toll and this house, like so many others, would soon collapse, rot, and disappear.

The windows had been broken out and an old bent back screen door banged against the side of the house when the wind blew. Curious, I was drawn to get a closer look. In back of the house sat a mounded area with an excavated staircase – the storm shelter. Every prairie home had one. It was where the family took cover when tornados approached. Peering in through the windows of the house I could see where large portions of the ceiling had fallen in. Over in the corner was the skeleton of a raccoon. Scattered about were pieces of broken furniture. In the middle of the floor was a woman's single shoe. I rested my hand on the window sill. The wood was weather beaten and dry. If I slid my hand along it, I could easily pick up splinters from the grayish colored pine.

So this was it, I thought. Except for some scattered tombstones, this was the only tangible reminder of one family's story – the struggle to come out west in search of opportunity in a place inhabited by Indians and roaming herds of buffalo. Their lives back East must have been some kind of miserable if coming to the wilderness of Kansas meant improvement. At first it must have been terribly difficult just to survive the bitter winters and the broiling summers. Then, the work required to establish a farm would have been exhausting and never ending – running a plow, digging a well, building fences, etc. Gradually it would have improved as these upland pilgrims grew accustomed to life on the Great Plains. The sod hut gave way to the log cabin which in turn was replaced by the forgotten structure now before me. They were free and independent. They prospered. Still, it would have been a very austere way of life by our standards. The forces of nature had ingrained in them a deep sense of sacrifice and humility.

Over time it all changed. The children grew up and moved away. Young men went off to war and never returned. The Dust Bowl days and the Great Depression destroyed much of what they had built. Then came the next big war. Men went to fight and women moved to the cities for factory jobs and a new way of life. Farming life was dull. When the lonely old husband and wife finally died, there was nobody who wanted the house. Farming methods had improved. The neighbor on the adjoining quarter section bought the land but he didn't need the house so it sat and deteriorated. This scenario has repeated itself over and over again. The value was always in the land.

By the end of the day it had grown warmer. We gathered around the vehicles for a beer and a review of the day's action. We were parked at the edge of a field on a high spot with a great view to the west and a sunset that grew more glorious with the approaching darkness. Kansas and the other Great Plains states truly were the land of the low horizon. Here, our planet sank under the weight of a winter sky that was deep orange with streaks of red and slashed with the vapor trails left behind by jets ferrying important types to and fro between New York and Los Angeles. Those travelers in the sky had no idea or concern about what we were doing. They looked down upon this great vastness as a nuisance that delayed them from serious matters on the coasts.

My hunting companions and I enjoyed the last moments of the day in the rich air, field dressing a mixed bag of quail and pheasant, divvying up the birds in plastic bags so we didn't have to fool with them later. It had grown dark. We loaded up the vehicle. Driving back to Kansas City, we listened to the NFL playoffs on the radio.

Chapter 28: Winter's Moan

I was at home on another Sunday afternoon. The world lay anesthetized by winter and we hibernated under a thick blanket of snow. The stillness led me to reflect. Once again, I thought about all these little children who died from cancer – deprived of a full life. Would Charlotte end up like them – shortchanged by time? If my daughter died in childhood, I wanted to make sure that my life would somehow compensate for her premature death. And if I were ever fortunate enough to accomplish anything significant, I would want to figure out some way to transfer the credit to her because her misfortune would have served as an inspiration for me to do more with my life.

And if she lived, would our grown children be connected to a loving network of family and friends after Deb and I were gone? Would they remember us with smiles? Would they tell their grandchildren about us? Would our children's children carry any of our traits? Would Whitney and Carter visit our graves or pass down my shotguns to their sons? Would a hearty pot of soup on the stove be a poignant reminder of Debbie? Would a formation of geese flying overhead make them think of me?

On January 11th, Charlotte had her first CT scan in two months. I was confident about it but Debbie was very nervous. With many other fellow patients, she had seen firsthand what happened when the cancer returned. Once again, we found ourselves in that state of uncertainty, hoping and praying that the scan results would test negative for cancer. We tried to stay busy to keep from worrying, but fear stalked us. And it would be like this for the next several years, I realized. We would live our lives in three month intervals – from checkup to checkup – until Charlotte made it to that magic five-year mark.

On January 14th, Debbie and I met with Dr. Freeman and Cathy Burks for a briefing on the meeting of the tumor board. We sat down in one of the examination rooms at the clinic where Charlotte went to have blood drawn when she wasn't staying on Four North.

"Hello, Kerr's. How's the busy family?"

"We're good, Doctor. Just hoping to make it through the home stretch."

"Once we determine the best approach on her radiation treatment we'll be that much closer."

Debbie interjected, "Doctor Freeman, we're anxious to hear what the tumor board decided. What's next?"

He sat back in his chair and adjusted his eyeglasses.

"It's the consensus of the board to go forward with radiation. However, the question is how do we best administer it? Do we give her 4,000 rads externally over five weeks or do we give her 2,000 rads intra-operatively and complete the dosage externally?"

"What's the hangup?" Debbie asked.

"It depends on whether Dr. Sharp thinks he can safely operate. The procedure is quite involved and it will generate even more scar tissue around her abdominal area."

"Seems pretty simple to me," I responded. "Go the external route."

"That has its risks too," said Burks. "External can damage the kidneys and vertebrae. If the vertebrae get hit, they stop growing. If two or three get hit, Charlotte could lose up to several inches in height as a full grown adult. It could limit her physically and give her abnormal posture. It might even lead to back surgery."

Debbie spoke up again: "So, Doctor Freeman, when do we find out what Sharp wants to do?"

"He's returning from vacation in the next several days. We'll know then. Anything else?"

"Tell us what to expect from the radiation itself. What side effects will show up?"

"Nothing you haven't seen already. It will cause nausea, fever, and loss of appetite. It's not as difficult as chemotherapy but," and he paused, "radiation could produce additional tumors as she grows older."

We looked around the room at each other and let it sink in.

"So be it," I thought to myself. Life is full of risks. Like everything else, extending Charlotte's life came at a price. And yet, there it was again – that pesky notion of Time. Day to day we measured it out and dispensed it. Sometimes we charged for it. Other times we just gave it away. We didn't think much about it until it had nearly run out, when we'd used up our allotted amount. Then it became the most precious commodity – the extra time we thought we had – at the moment we were supposed to die. The overtime of life, ending in sudden death.

Then I returned to the discussion.

"One more thing, Dr. Freeman. What's a rad?"

"Good question. And don't take this the wrong way but it's difficult to answer in layman's terms. A rad is basically an amount of exposure and the net effect is determined not only by the amount of radiation but also the time of exposure."

"I don't understand that at all," said Debbie.

"I don't either," I added. "But that's why we're here with you."

Freeman smiled.

"As you said earlier, we're on the home stretch."

It was bitterly cold the day we received the much anticipated CT scan report. It was negative for any new cancer
growth but the following week we needed to have an MRI to
make certain. I didn't understand why we couldn't just bypass
the CT scan and go straight to the MRI. If it wasn't definitive,
why did we bother with it? All it did was add another round
of anxiety to the process. Sharp really didn't want to operate
unless the MRI picked up something the CT scan missed. The
tension kept building. So many things were up in the air. Had
her cancer returned? If so, what then? Back to more chemo?
Would we move ahead with the radiation? And how would
we administer the radiation? Would Sharp have to operate
again? Deep down I sensed he didn't want to do it. Charlotte
had already had a very traumatic type of surgery. And radiation surgery would be no chip shot.

My head felt like it was in a vise. Sales and leases were usually slow after New Year's. It was especially bad this year. The
bill collectors called each night. American Express reminded
me that the January payment was late. North American Savings Bank wanted to know when we would get current on
our overdue mortgage payment. Mariella and the boys were
screaming. Whitney, still learning to walk, jostled a table in
the living room. The porcelain vase atop it wobbled and fell,
shattering in front of the fireplace. It was a gift from Debbie's
grandmother in Monterey, Mexico. The relentless cold and
snowy weather added another layer to our frustration.

Samantha, a five year old with neuroblastoma, relapsed.
Debbie had become good friends with Samantha's mother and
she broke down sobbing when she heard the news. Every
time another cancer patient died or relapsed, Debbie and I felt
it. That could just as easily have been Charlotte. It was hard
not to worry about it. Debbie sometimes thought that we and
Charlotte were going through this whole exercise with great
expectations which would be dashed in the end. With the
deaths of these other children, it seemed as if we were playing

a gruesome game of musical chairs but in this version, when the music stopped, someone died.

Chapter 29: Return of Hope

The weather had finally warmed up but it was rainy, wet, and dreary. The temperature was supposed to drop back down again, which would bring more sleet and snow. But we didn't care. Bring on a blizzard and it would not have bothered us. We felt happy because the MRI confirmed the results of the CT scan – no new evidence of cancer. It was such a huge relief. The fog of uncertainty melted away and step by step the final act of Charlotte's treatment plan came together. Since the MRI showed no trace of cancer, Sharp strongly recommended against surgery. Everyone agreed to go with the external treatment. It would be just as effective but without the greater risk of collateral damage as long as the radiation was on target. If we could make it through the radiation, we could resume a normal life.

Charlotte completed her first radiation treatment on January 26th. They told us that the side effects would not appear until after a week. Dr. Massey was the radiologist and she came highly recommended. Charlotte had to receive about five pinhead sized tattoos around her stomach which Massey used as reference points to make sure the radiation hit the bull's eye. She would receive treatment every weekday for five weeks at Trinity Lutheran Hospital, Massey's base of operations, which was just west of Mercy in an area of town nicknamed "Hospital Hill."

Early one morning I looked over at Debbie beside me. She was still asleep. I didn't yet feel like getting out of bed. I stretched and let my mind wander. I thought of springtime and how nice it would be when we were done with winter and Charlotte's cancer treatments. I imagined myself hunting for morel mushrooms.

There are certain parallels between children, cancer, and morels, I thought. Pushing their way up through the decay of the
past, they were new life and hope after a long period of cold
and gray. Morels sprang up early in the year just as Charlotte's
cancer had come early in life. Charlotte's cancer, like morels, was mysterious and rare. Morels and childhood cancer
sprouted randomly. Children and morels were a special blessing, but childhood – like morel season – was fleeting. And not
all mushrooms were good to eat. Some could be malignant,
like a cancerous tumor.

On our next hunt, we would find the largest group of morels
ever. They would surround us. We would have to be careful
where we stepped so as not to smash any of them. Charlotte
and Mariella would squeal and giggle as they plucked one
after another and deposited them in the bucket. After we had
picked several hundred, we would take the scenic route back
home to Kansas City along Highway 24.

On the north side of Lexington we would stop at the Mit-
tieville Peckerwood Club, which sat perched on a bluff over-
looking the Missouri River. It was an old roadhouse that served
up catfish, fried chicken, and mountain oysters. We'd sit at the
bar. I would order us all cheeseburgers and fries. The girls
would have milkshakes. It was a friendly place where Leon,
the bartender, would sit and visit, making sure that Charlotte
and Mariella were getting enough to eat.

We would arrive home by mid afternoon. I'd soak the morels in water before cooking. I would heat the butter, white
wine, shallots, and minced garlic. When it started to sizzle, I
would add the mushrooms, cut in half for soaking and cooking. The mixture would fill our kitchen with an earthy, se-
ductive aroma. Something really good was about to happen.
Mariella would try them but Charlotte might pass. These morels would be the most delicious ever. I would wash them
down with a gulp of chardonnay. Debbie would try a couple

and rave about how good they were. Both of the girls would be pleased with themselves for helping to find something that Mommy and Daddy really liked. Whitney and Carter wouldn't know what was going on, but our happiness was contagious, so they would smile too.

The sound of National Public Radio abruptly interrupted my reverie. The clock radio had gone off. There was another scandal story involving President Clinton. I didn't want to listen so I got up and headed off to the shower.

My upbeat feelings about Charlotte's treatment were reflected in a business windfall as well. Our company had been approached about merging with the biggest real estate firm in St. Louis, Turley Martin. They were much larger and very profitable. Their corporate client list was impressive and had grown even larger as big lending institutions hired them to lease and manage foreclosures in the wake of the savings and loan crisis. My father and I saw several reasons why it made sense. First, he and I both preferred to work on transactions. Neither of us liked administrative work nor were we good at it. The merger would allow us to focus on brokerage. Secondly, merging with Turley Martin instantly took us to another level. We'd been a respected mom and pop operation but had been shut out of doing business with certain institutions. Not any longer. The merger would put us in an organization with offices worldwide. We were also planning to move out of the Brookfield Building into the iconic Power and Light Building which we had just taken over as a new management account.

We added one more change: Debbie and I contracted to buy a new house in Prairie Village, Kansas, across State Line Road. Kansas ... I never thought I'd move across the state line but with Charlotte starting kindergarten next year, we figured it was the best alternative. In a sense, it was our act of faith in Charlotte's full recovery because we were moving out of Missouri to be in the better school system in Kansas.

Chapter 30: Radioactive

On Wednesday, February 2nd, I took Charlotte to her daily radiation regimen at Trinity Lutheran. It was my first time to see Charlotte go through the treatment but after a week's worth, Charlotte was an old hand at it. We played around in the waiting room until the technician summoned us. The room we entered was large with high ceilings. Against the north wall was a tall box-shaped piece of equipment that had an attachment – shaped like a telephone receiver – protruding out into the room. Each end could swivel around the table on which the patient would receive the radiation. The table itself was like an altar. It could raise or lower itself mechanically as recumbent patients lay there in total vulnerability ready to receive the sacrament of radiation. Against the walls were boxes which housed lasers. These helped aim the radiation beams. Charlotte, like every other patient, had her own personalized flat, square piece of metal that the technician inserted into the radiation device like a cookie sheet, as a protection for the vital organs. As they prepared for the session, I removed her shirt and then helped her climb onto the table. With her Hickman dangling to the side, she reclined into the plastic mold shaped specifically to her little body. The red laser lights ran across her torso at several angles. In the darkened room, the red of the laser lines seemed eerily bright. At this point, Charlotte put on her serious face and became silent so as to preserve her motionless state.   She'd been told this was important. With the final adjustments completed, I had to leave the treatment area for the control room where I could watch Charlotte via a video monitor. She stayed perfectly still as the technician pushed buttons and administered the treatment in a matter of seconds.

As expected, Charlotte fell ill from the radiation after only one and a half weeks of it. She had been vomiting and had diarrhea. Debbie worried that she might have an intestinal blockage. The other worry was that we had to watch her blood counts closely. There was a very good chance they would drop. We had a tough three weeks ahead as Charlotte struggled to reach the finish line. And what a time it was to head down the home stretch. February was always the worst month of the year in Kansas City. Outside the temperature was two degrees above zero with a 20-below wind chill. Despite her discomfort, Charlotte had recently developed a strong appreciation for rock and roll music. I think it came from her cousins Regan and Erin. It was a good sign that she could find something to raise her spirits.

Whitney and Carter had their one year checkups at Dr. Mitra's. Although they both had hit the lower end of the percentile for height and weight, they were doing fine. Personality wise, Whitney seemed more sensitive and affectionate. Carter seemed more independent. They both were happy and full of energy. My mother said Mariella had beautiful behavior when she watched her one day. I observed the same when I surprised Mariella at her preschool as the "helper." The parents each took turns showing up to spend time with a child. The look on her face was priceless. It made her feel good to have Dad in class with her. Also, we had given Mariella the responsibility of feeding our dog, Punky, every morning. She was excited about the new duty. It made her feel grown up. We would need her help. Big changes were coming on the home front.

The bigger concern at this point was Charlotte. We had to check her into Four North for observation because of stomach cramps, continued diarrhea, and dropping blood counts. I stopped in to see her in the evening. She was very quiet. I could tell she was sad for having to be there. I asked Charlotte if she would like to have her classmates call her on the phone. She didn't want them to call. I felt so badly for her and hoped that she could return home soon. We sat together and watched "The Wizard of Oz" holding hands. When the movie ended and I rose to head home, she grabbed on to me. She didn't want me to go.

I glumly walked down the corridor towards the parking garage. How many times had Debbie and I made this trip? Coming in and going out – sometimes with Charlotte, but more often without. Those long passageways kept us connected to her until we reached the doors. But when we walked outside, we separated ourselves and left the world of Four North. We hated the feeling of leaving her behind and wondered why we couldn't somehow switch places with her and do the suffering ourselves. How many more times, I wondered, would I have to leave her this way?   "Sleep well, Charlotte," I thought as I got in the car.

Chapter 31: Goodbye, Mr. Hickman

After taking the children to inspect the new house, we went on our first family restaurant outing with Whitney and Carter. Our destination was Tippin's Restaurant at Corinth Shopping Center. The place was known for its delicious pies. They may never let us return. Mariella and Charlotte were not on their best behavior, acting loud and fussy. The boys were hungry and uncontrollable. Tippin's attracted a sizeable number of the geriatric set from nearby "Wrinkle City" and other residential "communities" geared to the older crowd. As the children made their presence known, we received quite a number of unappreciative stares from the elderly customers. Food and silverware were scattered all over the floor and glasses of water and milk were spilled repeatedly. When mixed with the crumbled crackers, the water and milk created a glue-like paste made worse by the addition of paper napkins. This grody sludge worked its way into the carpet. Loud screams and whining continued to punctuate the noisy clatter of spoons and dishes as our meal drew to an end. It wasn't particularly enjoyable, but when we stood to leave I had to suppress a laugh. It was an awful mess and I was glad we were away from home. I left a nice tip because of the cleanup job we left them – and also for the prompt service. Once they realized the unruliness of our group, they decided to turn our table as quickly as possible.

Our departure was a relief to everyone present and maybe it was my imagination, but for a moment I sensed pity in their faces as we left – similar to the way people look at a handicapped person – as if it's abnormal or not quite right in the head to have a large family of little children. Or perhaps they were just glad not to be in our shoes. Sometimes I thought that Deb and I were losing our minds, but I would never trade places with the lonely old people spending their last days shuffling around Tippin's. I'd rather take the mass confusion that comes with four children. That was an easy choice because we had the prospects of a good future. We were young and had a lot of life ahead of us. And Charlotte had regained her health. She was feeling so much better. Her appetite had returned along with normal body functions. It was amazing to see her recovery.

The following Sunday at church, I heard one of the finest sermons ever. Perhaps it struck me because of the situation with Charlotte. As we were in late February, it was relevant for the Lenten season, a time of renewal. In old English, Lent meant "Spring." The subject of the sermon was the Cross as a symbol. The guest preacher was Father Kenneth Leech, an Anglican priest from East London, England. Renowned for his speaking and writing, Leech talked about how, during this time of renewal as Christians, we must not fall prey to distorted views of what the Cross represents. One was that which sought to use the Cross as a weapon with which to harass or beat people over the head. This brought to mind some of the ultra evangelical, Bible banging, born again types. The other distortion was the one which looked at the Cross as a sort of gloomy call to obedience which required an ascetic, sometimes masochistic lifestyle – one of sacrifice and suffering in order to do the Lord's work, not unlike certain monastic orders of the Roman Catholic Church. As I understood Leech's message, the two distortions were at rather opposite ends of the religious spectrum. One used the Cross as a weapon to inflict upon "sinful" people, the other used it to inflict pain and suffering on oneself. But according to Leech, the correct way to interpret the Cross was as a symbol of hope. No matter our imperfections, no matter how difficult life became, God loved us. If we held to this belief, He would take care of us. Here and hereafter. It was a simple yet powerful message and one that I saw as reinforcement of my own religious views. It also fit in nicely with the healing and renewal taking place with Charlotte.

But the healing process wasn't always an upward curve. It had its dips along the way. At least we had made it through the month of February. Charlotte had to go back into the main hospital as a result of complications from the recently-resumed radiation. They thought she might have contracted hepatitis. We would not know what type or anything for another couple of days. Once again, Deb and I were apart. Deb was at the hospital and I was holding down the fort at home. Charlotte had improved quite a bit from when she doubled over in pain nearly giving our nanny, Laree, a heart attack.

One day, we had beautiful 73-degree weather and clear skies. Deb, Mariella, Whitney, Carter, and I had a picnic in Loose Park. Decent weather had been long overdue. It was still a bit too early to celebrate springtime, but we could taste it.

We still didn't know what type of hepatitis Charlotte had, but Freeman decided to stop the radiation treatment with the dosage about eighty percent complete. The radiation had hit her hard. Then Charlotte would have her Hickman removed and she would step into that oncological purgatory between remission and a clean bill of health. Between regular blood tests, CT scans, and MRIs, we should be through the worst of it in about five years – God willing.

Have we done everything we could? Have we pushed Charlotte to the absolute limits of her ability to handle any more treatment? I felt comfortable answering "Yes." All of us had serious doubts about giving Charlotte any more chemo or radiation. Each time we did it, it hit her harder and more quickly. The lows reached closer and closer to the danger zone. Why tempt fate?

On March 25th, Sharp removed Charlotte's Hickman catheter. Her high maintenance appendage was finally gone. So was the cancer to the best of our knowledge. The worst of our ordeal had finally come to an end. I sensed a powerful urge to move on and put some distance between then and what had happened over the previous year. Our family needed to get past this and return to a normal life. At the same time, I didn't think I could ignore it or forget it. It had made us stronger emotionally and more appreciative for what we had. Never again would I look at Charlotte and fail to see her toughness, or at Debbie and fail to see her strength of spirit and love for the children.

Meanwhile, the weather kept improving. The deathly and difficult winter had faded away. We sold our house and some commission checks finally came in. Suddenly, we had so much more for which to be thankful. I wondered to myself – what did it? How did we get to this point when so many others came up short? Although it wouldn't be certain for several years, Charlotte had all the makings of a survivor. What did Mitra, Sharp, Freeman, the staff at Mercy, or we do that helped Charlotte get to this point? More and more people talked about the scientific data supporting prayer as a means of treating illness.

Atheists may snicker when they hear such claims. Let them. Atheism seems so cynical. And a cynical life doesn't seem to offer much happiness – just emptiness near as I can tell. We believed prayer played a major role in the outcome of Charlotte's case. So many people in the community and around the country had prayed for her. When it started, we had no proven treatment for curing her disease. Her survival had been miraculous.

Organized religion has been a cause of great strife throughout the ages but not with Charlotte's illness. We were Episcopalians, Mitra was a Hindu, Sharp was a Mormon, and Freeman was an Orthodox Jew. Maybe this was some kind of ecumenical collaboration meant to serve as an example to humanity that we could overcome our differences and work together and do good things. It certainly worked well in Charlotte's case.

On April 2nd we celebrated Easter. The air was crisp with clear blue skies. Although it was chilly, the day was appropriately glorious and not a cloud in the sky. We had our Easter egg hunt in the back yard. Because of the cool weather, we all wore bathrobes. Later, at the Cathedral, Charlotte and Mariella looked adorable in their Easter dresses. Mariella wore a straw hat. Whitney and Carter looked very handsome with their blue and white outfits and fresh crew cuts. Easter gave us hope – especially this year, having finished a difficult chapter in our lives. That day, for us, was also a special celebration of resurrection – not only from death but also from cancer.

Chapter 32: Dream Factory

Debbie, Charlotte, Mariella, and I boarded a US Airways flight to Orlando. We were headed to Disney World, courtesy of the Dream Factory. The girls were very excited. We stayed at Kids Village at Kissimmee, a resort dedicated to young children with life threatening illnesses. The entertainment area was inside a castle which looked like something out of a storybook. The dining area was a gingerbread house on the exterior. Each family had its own bungalow.

Kids Village had all the amenities one could imagine – a nice swimming pool that was wheelchair accessible, a playground, and a fishing pond with a play boat in it. The pond was stocked with catfish. Apparently, turtles and alligators had crashed the party on occasion – no doubt because of the abundant supply of fat and slow moving fish – made so by the daily supply of leftovers and scraps from the gingerbread house.

Except for a small paid staff – Kids Village was run by volunteers – many of them were elderly retirees. Florida had a good supply of this resource. They were all very kind and had that special disposition which is difficult to replicate in paid employees. These volunteers wanted to be there and they loved to be around children. The Board of Directors was very impressive and read like a Who's Who of Hollywood and Corporate America.

The families who visited Kids Village came from all over the world. We befriended one man, Alan, from Dublin, Ireland, who was with his terminally ill five-year-old son. There were families from as far away as France and Israel. Childhood diseases like cancer also covered the social spectrum. Childhood cancer didn't discriminate. It hit rich and poor alike.

One day, as I sat by the pool letting the warm sun dry me after a swim, I watched a couple in the pool with their child. The little boy was severely handicapped. He appeared unable to move any of his limbs. He couldn't even hold up his head. His parents looked so tired. I had noticed them earlier in a dilapidated handicap conversion van. The father wore old blue jeans and a faded work shirt with the kind of tan that comes from physical work outdoors. His wife looked haggard in an old print dress that draped over her like a bag. They were in the pool with their clothes on. They had no swimsuits. But there was powerful beauty in their unconditional love for a sick child. It was a scene I would never forget. All I could see or think about was their patience and devotion to a child who had no chance for any kind of a normal life. It was obvious that their child's care had taken a heavy toll on them, but at that moment, as they swept him around the pool, they were smiling and happy. Together as a family.

Using Kids Village as our base camp, we visited Disney World, MGM Studios, The Magic Kingdom, and Sea World. Mariella and Charlotte absolutely loved it. It was nice to see Mariella enjoying herself after the difficult year we had had. Mariella and Charlotte saw many of their favorite Disney characters such as Snow White, Aladdin, Jasmine, Goofy, Chip and Dale, and Mickey and Minnie Mouse. We went on rides, took lots of pictures, and enjoyed the sights and sounds of this children's paradise. Sea World was more interesting to me as it offered all types of marine life versus cartoon characters, but this trip wasn't geared to what I like. We were here for Charlotte and Mariella. The Dream Factory people told us that our trip invitation had nothing to do with financial wherewithal. They offered trips regardless of the family's ability to pay. It was very generous of the organization to do this for us and it meant so much to Charlotte and Mariella.

Disneyland was already crowded and it was early in the season. Fortunately, we had a special badge which allowed Charlotte and Mariella to cut in line. Some people would wait 45 to 60 minutes for a ride. I didn't think I could do that in July when it topped 100 degrees, when bodies were packed together, dripping in sweat with tempers edging up as people pushed and shoved to get their kids in front of Mickey Mouse and Donald Duck.

Back in Kansas City, winter's last gasp offered rain and a 40ish temperature. When we arrived in Orlando, it was stormy, but eventually the sun came out the temperature was in the 80's. I'd almost forgotten what real humidity felt like. But it would get better in Kansas City soon. Turkey season was approaching along with the other things we enjoyed during springtime

– crappie fishing and fresh morels. But there was one thing about the new season we didn't enjoy – dangerous weather.

Chapter 33: Tornado Warning

The worst tornadoes often began on a nice day. It would be sunny and warm. You could feel the humidity rise until it got breezy. The humidity would return when the wind died down. As the day wore on, the wind blew harder and you sensed a gradual drop in the temperature. At that point you realized, as a native, that bad weather was on the way. But then you shrugged to yourself and thought – oh well, that's what happens this time of year. Besides, the farmers need the rain.

That's the way it was on April 28th. I'd read the forecast in the paper calling for late afternoon thunderstorms. I'd also heard about it on the radio. But it didn't worry me.

Tornadoes didn't come through the city anymore. They hit the rural areas. They especially liked trailer parks. When they didn't angrily obliterate mobile homes, they curiously peeled them open like sardine cans and scattered their contents in every direction. I vaguely remembered hearing why tornadoes didn't come into the city. The scientific explanation was that it had something to do with the urban heat repelling and pushing them away like the beefy doorman at a trendy nightclub. Tornadoes didn't make the list. With their bizarre behavior, they simply were not welcome.

So we went about our business – not worried about the approaching storm. The weather reports on TV and radio took on a more serious tone. There was a massive front to the southwest involving heavy thunderstorms and potential tornadoes moving our direction. Our weather almost always came from the southwest. Only three years prior, an enormous super cell spawned sixty-nine tornadoes which ravaged the Wichita area destroying hundreds of homes and killing twenty people.

By late afternoon it started to sprinkle and grew dark. It felt much cooler as I left the office and walked over to the Barney Allis parking garage. When I arrived home, the rain was pouring down. Debbie and the girls were excited to see me. Charlotte and Mariella bounced around like they needed to go potty. They informed me that we were under a severe thunderstorm warning and a tornado watch. About an hour west near Ottawa, KS., were unconfirmed reports of tornadoes on the ground. The TV weather reporters interrupted regular programming as the nasty storm approached the metro area.

Ominous clouds were spotted around Lawrence and DeSoto, still headed our way. The rain had stopped. Suddenly the tornado sirens began to wail. They were very loud and eerie at the same time. For some strange reason, I was reminded of London during World War II. Above us the sky was dark gray, but to the west it was darker and menacing. I didn't remember seeing uglier clouds. They were roiling and angry like a bubbling pot of black bean soup. Our dog, Punky, started barking hysterically, but at what I didn't know. Maybe the change in barometric pressure hurt his ears.

What if we did get a tornado? It had been so long since one came through town. The infamous Ruskin Heights tornado of 1957 killed more than 50 people. In its aftermath, the pictures of smashed houses looked like little piles of matchsticks. After that was Topeka in 1966. It went through the middle of town and leveled Washburn University. A lot of people died.

Debbie and I rounded up some blankets, a flashlight, and an old transistor radio. We took the children to the basement. The experts said we should go to that corner of the cellar closest to the oncoming storm. In our case, that was the southwest corner. The theory was that the tornado will come in like a sweeping broom and pass over an area just under that first edge of the basement making one's chances of survival much greater than if one huddled up in the far corner where one was more likely to get swept up along with all the other debris.

I scanned the basement. Along the south wall was an extra mattress we could pull over us for better protection. What kills people in tornadoes more than anything else is the junk turned shrapnel flying through the air at more than 100 miles per hour. If it hit you, you were in big trouble. Tornadoes did weird things. We had heard the freakish stories of wheat straw stuck in trees or pitchforks piercing a washtub. Keep your head down and cover up. Hope you don't get sucked up into the vortex.

I looked over at Debbie and the children. Earlier today I had scoffed at the idea of a tornado threatening us. But after seeing the malevolent skies approaching us, I was a believer. Then I was struck by the irony of going through all we had over the past year, only to get wiped out and perish in a tornado. Who said life was fair?

We now heard the rat-a-tat-tat of hail bouncing off windows and metallic surfaces. Hail and tornadoes moved in tandem like drunken ballroom dancers madly twirling around, crashing into tables, and knocking other couples out of their way. The survivors often said that when it finally came, it roared like 100 freight trains barreling down the track. It never did. As the treacherous clouds approached the city, the funnels retracted.

And then it was over. The storm had passed. Slowly, we and our neighbors emerged from our homes and stepped out to survey the damage. Other than a few branches on the ground, everything looked fine. It was still and quiet. No breeze at all. To the west, the sun was shining through a magnificent rainbow. We were going to be okay.

Chapter 34: Beyond the RTC

I was in flight returning to Kansas City from Washington D.C. where I attended the Society of Industrial and Office Realtors Spring Convention. The meeting was productive. George

Will addressed us on the breakdown of the American family
and the myriad urban problems resulting from the same. I
had been getting better acquainted with the other members of
the Society. That was essential in order to make my member-
ship worthwhile. It was very helpful to trade information with
brokers from other parts of the country to see how Kansas
City compared to other markets. The ultimate goal was to
refer business back and forth. Overall, the mood of the group
was positive. Many believed we were finally emerging from
the depressed conditions of the past several years. Big inves-
tors, with a national scope, were buying large portfolios of
property. Across the country, ownership was becoming more
institutional and the small, local investor was less of a factor.
The dominant trend we noticed was the collectivism of ownership. It was what the consultants called "a new paradigm."
Those with lots of cash or the collateral to borrow now ruled
the roost. But the good news was that, as brokers, we had
transactions to work on. And in many cases, these deals could
be substantial.

On the flight home I looked out the window of the plane as
we sailed over the clouds and the land far below. At 35,000
feet I saw a ribbon-like waterway. From this distance it seemed
like nothing more than a capillary, a small contributor to a
larger vessel farther down the drainage basin where there was
a major river.

The savings and loan crisis had been an economic disaster
on the same order of magnitude as the Missouri River deluge
the previous summer. In those frantic days, we stood watch at
Case Park and looked down upon the source of her madness,
the swollen intrusion of the Kaw. We prayed for the levees
to hold. At the same time, we tumbled along in a torrent
of our own economic madness. All of us connected to the
real estate business were awash in it. There were charlatans
who got flushed out when they couldn't make debt service.
Their projects were ill conceived and stupid. In many cases,

the principals were simply crooks. There were lenders who knew better than to make some of the loans they did. But what gnawed at my sense of fairness were the decent people who were still current on their loans. Their only mistake was to have borrowed from the wrong savings and loan. Now we realized how one sided the lending process had become. The onus was always on the borrowers to prove their creditworthiness.

Nobody ever thought to question the lender until it was too late. Like a weak levee, their lenders busted wide open and the decent folks got swept away, washed into a pool of good and bad loans managed by the distant bureaucrats of the Resolution Trust Corporation. The RTC solution was to dump a bunch of black suited sharks into the pool. The good borrowers were treated like chum. The water roiled and turned red. But the RTC didn't care. The loan tank was bulging. It needed thinning out.

So the sharks bought the loans at deep discounts, full well knowing the current borrowers couldn't refinance, much less pay them off at full face value. When the sharks foreclosed, they ended up owning the properties for ten and 20 cents on the dollar. Some of the honest people lost a lifetime's worth of work. Huge fortunes were made. Certain economists claimed this event would stand as one of the greatest transfers of wealth in the history of our country.

The highlight of the Washington, D.C., trip was a visit to the National Gallery of Art. The excellent collection ranged from pre-Renaissance to the present, including the portrait of Ginevra de' Benci, Leonardo da Vinci's only work in the United States. "The Jolly Flatboatmen," one of George Caleb Bingham's best known works, was prominently displayed. Bingham was from, of all places, Arrow Rock, Missouri.

I'm not sure why, but several portraits of women made a big impression on me. John Singer Sargent's "Repose," Gainsborough's "Mrs Sheridan," and Thomas Eakin's portrait of Harriet

Husson Carville all had a haunting beauty. The lovely subjects of all these paintings were long since deceased, but in a way they lived on in the canvass. Those paintings made me think of Debbie and the engagement picture I kept of her at my office. In the photo, she glows contentedly at our upcoming nuptials. We'd been through so much together since then, and especially this past year. I appreciated her more now than ever. Her devotion to our children – and especially to Charlotte during the treatment – was extraordinary. In those moments when it seemed like things couldn't be worse, she was at her best.

My favorite painting was "Child in a Straw Hat" by Mary Cassatt. It reminded me so much of Charlotte. The subject's expression was all too familiar – caught in that moment before she sputtered and fussed or broke into an impish grin; the embodiment of what it meant to have a child. Sadness and joy all mixed together.

Chapter 35: Resumption

May 8th marked a year since Charlotte fell ill. It would be our last chance of the season to find morels. Our hunt started out slowly. We were having no luck. The new spring foliage was thick and lush, dripping from a combination of heavy dew and overnight rain. This time water raced along the normally quiet creek which cut through our forested morel patch. A broken eggshell caught my eye. It was larger than a chicken egg and had tiny brown speckles. Charlotte, Mariella, and I examined it and realized it was a turkey egg. We moved on slowly scanning the ground for mushrooms when, not more than ten feet away and with a terrific rustling noise, up burst a big hen turkey. She flew off through the woods like a lumbering old B-52 bomber. Recovered from our momentary surprise, we walked over to the spot where she had lifted off. There beneath the brush were ten turkey eggs neatly grouped in a circle.

The discovery of the nest was a first for me and the girls. I had never seen a turkey nest before. The eggs seemed so vulnerable there on the ground, subject to weather and the predations of skunks, raccoons, and possums.

"Oh Daddy, please let us take them home."

"Daddy, we want them."

I did my best to explain to the girls that this was how new turkeys come into the world. They both begged me to let them take the eggs with us back to Kansas City. I resisted, explaining that they were better off in the wild.

"Girls, if we want these turkey eggs to live, they need to stay right here with their mama. She'll come back after we're gone. We should leave them alone. That's how it works in nature. That's the way it's supposed to be. If we take 'em home, they'll die. C'mon now. We don't want that, do we?"

Mariella looked up at me, "Daddy, I don't want 'em to die. I like turkeys."

"Me too, Dad," said Charlotte.

"Good. You girls are doin' what's best. So, why don't we head over this away. I'm still waitin' on one 'a you to find a morel. Remember, first one gets a dollar."

In their young minds it didn't make sense that our abandonment of the eggs gave them a better chance of survival. We always go to great lengths to protect the lives of those we love. Yet most of the time, their well being is out of our control. Nature and God above have the final say.

The right thing was to leave those eggs alone. And so we did.

Charlotte (Cheerleader.)

EPILOGUE

October 25, 2010

It was a gorgeous Saturday afternoon in late October as I sat in the historic stands of Francis Field at Washington University in St. Louis. I was there to see Charlotte cheerlead for the Bears football team as they went up against the Battling Bishops of Ohio Wesleyan.

The air was autumn crisp and the sky was clear blue. Yellow leaves fell from the trees behind the stadium and blew over the spectators out onto the field. The home team pep band added spirit to the occasion, and I watched Charlotte go through her cheer routines with watery eyes. I thought about how far we had come since that fateful morel hunt 17 years ago in the spring of 1993.

So many things have happened since then. Our world is a much different place due to advances in technology and the specter of terrorism. Many we knew are no longer here. Those of us left carry the baggage of time and, mindful of our own mortality, we see the future in the lives of our children.

An older friend once commented that he didn't really think about his own mortality until his first child was born. I didn't experience it quite that way. It hit me later in life. The thought of my own passing didn't come until my children went off to college. I think about it more these days – not so much out of fear but in bewilderment.

My late uncle Frank from Memphis used to say, "Tempus sho' do fugit." (Time flies.) How right he was. Between the span of Charlotte's illness when I kept a raggedy journal and now as I put the finishing touches on this book, my children have grown up and left the nest. One piece of advice I'll share: Don't get to this stage in life and realize you didn't spend enough time with your children. You'll never get it back.

Some have suggested that I pass on a few of the things I learned from Charlotte's illness. I'm happy to do so and would only add that these pointers apply to parents of any seriously sick child – not just cancer patients. From a practical standpoint, maintain health insurance for your family. Whatever sacrifices you must make to have health insurance, make them. It could turn out to be your best investment ever. Secondly, children's best advocates are their parents. Get a second opinion and don't be afraid to challenge the experts. Ask questions. Even if you don't feel comfortable, speak up, because nobody else will. At the same time, show appreciation to your children's caregivers. Their jobs are difficult on so many levels. Finally, at some point in life your children or those of someone close to you will need a place like Children's Mercy Hospital. As citizens, we contribute to so many things in our communities – sports, entertainment, culture, etc. We must never forget to support children's hospitals.

From an emotional perspective, I would say to parents of sick children the following: Family and friends go unappreciated until times of crisis. When the chips are down, you find out who really cares about you and your family. And, none of us have cornered the market on suffering. There's always someone worse off than you. Also, as difficult as it may get, don't ignore your other children and your spouse. They need your love too. If worrying ever solved any problems, the world would be a perfect place. Don't get consumed with worry. The stress it causes will only make matters worse.

Dealing with serious illness is a huge dose of humility. One minute we're flying high and the next we realize how fragile life really is. But humility isn't all bad. It force feeds the soul. Without it we really cannot feel grateful for the good things in life. Lastly, when things are at their absolute worst, and they will get that way more than once, there's always our faith in God and the hope it provides. The ugliness of our world reminds us that in spite of all our progress in science and technology, life on earth will never be perfect. Remember this and you'll find that as awful as things can get, they will get better, especially in the hereafter.

And where are they now?

Charlotte graduated from Washington University in St. Louis with a double major in Business and Fashion Design. She has moved to Dallas and begun her career with Neiman Marcus in their Executive Development Program. She lives with the "late effects" of surviving childhood cancer. Some of these include an exceptionally low heart rate, occasional numbness in her extremities, and several benign tumors in her liver. None of these prevent her from leading an active and happy life. We've talked more than once about how she is so fortunate to have had a second chance at life. She owes it to herself and especially to all those fellow patients who didn't survive to make the most of her opportunities in life. So far I'd say she's done an excellent job of it. Debbie and I are very proud of her.

Mariella is doing very well in her senior year at Loyola of Chicago. When I talk to her now, I hear a young adult on the other end of the line. She has really blossomed. Her childhood curiosity is opening doors in many different directions. She loves music, photography, and ornithology. Her knowledge of birds is amazing. Debbie and I no longer feel the guilt of not having given her the attention we felt she deserved more of as a toddler. They told us when Charlotte was sick that these little children are resilient and that they do not suffer psychologically as a result of having cancer. The same holds true for Mariella. She's doing just fine.

Whitney III has turned into a very independent and self-sufficient young man. He has developed a passion for art and plans to attend the Memphis College of Art this fall. He graduated from Shawnee Mission East High School this past spring.

Carter also graduated from Shawnee Mission East High School this past spring. He resembles me in stature – short and stocky. He, like his brother Whitney, was a varsity wres-

tler. He plans to attend Kansas State this fall to study agriculture. Both Whitney and Carter have shown the ability to work
hard and to stand up for themselves. I look at all my children
and feel optimistic about the potential for the next generation.
Granted, they've had their share of mishaps along the way, but
they are smart and very capable.

Debbie and I will celebrate our 25th anniversary next May.
Charlotte's cancer experience definitely made our marriage
stronger. The trials we share with others have a way of con-
necting us more deeply. I appreciate some of Debbie's quali-
ties more so now than when Charlotte was sick. She knows
and understands our children. Her ability to perceive what it
is that drives each one of them is very helpful when dealing
with their problems. Her generosity knows no limits. I get
frustrated because she spreads herself too thin at times. She
never can say "no" when a friend or relative needs help. I'm
very lucky to have her as my wife.

My parents enjoy good health and spend nearly every weekend in Arrow Rock. They love it there. Their work on historic
preservation has resulted in lots of recognition. Bon Appetit
magazine featured our typical Thanksgiving gathering at Prairie Park in the November 2001 issue, and earlier this year my
parents received the Missouri Preservation Rozier Award pre-
sented at the state capitol in Jefferson City. My father still offices next to me and is active in the real estate business. In 1994
we officially merged Kerr & Company with Turley Martin out
of St. Louis. The new entity has grown to more than 60 cities
and is now known as Cassidy Turley. The change has been
good. Dad and I no longer worry about administrative matters. Now, all we do is focus on brokerage – he does land and
I concentrate on industrial properties, mainly warehouses.

Rick Ramos died on September 1st this year. His health had
deteriorated after a series of strokes. He passed away peace-
fully surrounded by Sally, Debbie, and the other siblings. His
death affected many people, especially Debbie and our chil-

dren. They loved him very much. And so did I. He was so helpful to us throughout Charlotte's illness, particularly during the early stages – the most traumatic part. The first person to show up and pay his respects at the funeral home was Charlie Wald.

Charlie told Debbie, "I'm here because your father saved my life."

Rick operated on Charlie back in the 1970s. The techniques he used in Charlie's case were quite radical but Charlie's still here today. Family man, surgeon, teacher, intellectual, gastronome extraordinaire ... I could go on and on. We will sorely miss him.

Sally copes as best as she can with her loss. I can't imagine how difficult it is to lose a spouse of more than 50 years. We stay in close touch with her.

I have no doubt it was God's will that Charlotte survived and a large part of that manifested itself in the doctors and staff at Children's Mercy Hospital. Although he was not affiliated with CMH at that time, Dr. Mitra first steered us there and made sure we linked up with Dr. Sharp. Dr. Mitra was a remarkable man and a brilliant physician. He knew right away that Charlotte's situation was very serious. Sadly, he passed away last year but he still saw patients well into his 80's. We will always be grateful to him for his care.

We have heard that Dr. Sharp has slowed down a little bit and doesn't maintain the grueling schedule he did when Charlotte was diagnosed. I only hope the young surgeons of today have the same level of determination he did. At one of the most critical moments of our ordeal, when we needed a miracle, God sent us Dr. Sharp. When I think of all the difficult procedures he completed over the course of his career and then compare them to my life's accomplishments, I feel very humbled.

Cathy Burks was the unsung heroine of our time at Mercy. Steady, constant, and so dependable, she helped us keep our

sanity during the most difficult times. When we think of the
dedicated staff at Mercy, she's the first who comes to mind. She
has continued to be a wonderful resource to us, our friends,
and family. We love you, Cathy Burks.

The last time I saw Dr. Freeman was in the summer of 1994
when we invited him and his wife to our home for dinner. As
an Orthodox Jew, he agreed to come provided that we serve
a kosher meal. There was a kosher market in Overland Park
at 95th and Nall Avenue named Jacobsens'. They were very
helpful and set us up with everything we needed including
kosher utensils and wine. That same year Dr. and Mrs. Freeman emigrated to Israel to live on a kibbutz.

I wonder what he's like today. I can imagine him there in the
medical clinic of a kibbutz, almost 20 years older, stooped and
frail. He gazes out a window across the neatly planted fields,
which gradually give way in the distance to rocky hills. He's
led a good full life.

The nurse interrupts his meditations.

"Dr. Freeman, your patient with the abdominal tumor is here
for the consultation."

"Oh yes, of course. Please send her in."

A little girl about five years old is ushered into the room accompanied by her parents. They are farming people from the
neighboring village. The father stands, nervously clutching his
hat with both hands.

"Dr. Freeman, they tell us you've worked a lot with these
stomach tumors. Can you help our daughter?"

Freeman focuses on the little girl.

"Come child. Come close so I can get a better look at you."

He gently puts his hands on her shoulders and looks into
her eyes. She returns the gaze, unafraid. "What is your name,
child?"

"Charlotte."

He continues smiling until the recognition hits him with a
delayed reaction. He blinks and leans back in his chair.

"Charlotte, you say? I once treated another girl named Charlotte. She was about your age, too."

He pauses for a moment and looks again out the window. This time his gaze carries beyond the hills to the west. He smiles and turns back to the parents.

"Yes. I can help your child. I can help Charlotte."

I wish I could share this story with Dr. Freeman but sadly, the hospital has lost touch with him. The man we didn't like at first but grew to love is now a mystery – much like the disease he was so passionate about fighting. If you're still out there, Dr. Freeman, thanks again for your determination and commitment to curing our daughter.